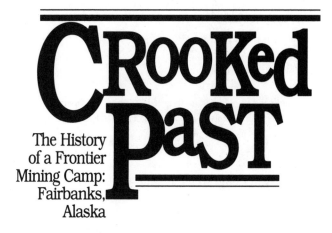

CROOKED PAST

The History
of a Frontier
Mining Camp:
Fairbanks,
Alaska

Terrence Cole

University of Alaska Press
Fairbanks, Alaska 1991

University of Alaska Press reprints: 1991, 1995, 1999, 2003
        PO Box 756240
        Fairbanks, AK 99775-6240
        fypress@uaf.edu
        www.uaf.edu/uapress

Originally published by Alaska Northwest Publishing Company as
E.T. Barnette: The Strange Story of the Man Who Founded Fairbanks,
first edition 1981, second edition 1984.

Library of Congress Cataloging-in-Publication Data
Cole, Terrence, 1953–
        [E.T. Barnette]
        Crooked past : a history of a frontier gold town
Fairbanks, Alaska / Terrence Cole.
        p. cm.
Reprint. Originally published: E.T. Barnette. 2nd ed.
Anchorage, Alaska : Alaska Northwest Pub. Co. 1984
Includes bibliographical references and index.
        1. Barnette, E. T. (Elbridge Truman) 2. Fairbanks (Alaska)--His-
tory. 3. Swindlers and swindling--Alaska--Fairbanks--Biography. I. Title.
F914.F16B375 1991
979.8'6--dc20   LOC: 91-4024
[B]   CIP
International Standard Book Number: 0-912006-53-6

Printed in the United States of America.
This publication was printed on paper that meets the minimum requirements
for ANSI/NISO z39.48-1992 (Permanence of Paper).

Book design by Dianne Hofbeck.
Cover design by Dixon Jones, UAF Rasmuson Library.

*Front cover: A rugged looking crew on Cleary Creek eyes the photographer before
riding down to the bottom of the mine shaft in a bucket attached to a steam hoist.
(University of Alaska Archives, Margaret Lentz Collection.)*

Contents

Acknowledgments

I would like to thank the staff of the Rasmuson Library for their generous assistance, especially those in the University of Alaska Archives, Renee Blahuta, Beverly Davis, and Paul McCarthy, and Patricia Sackinger in the newspaper room. Among the many people at the University of Alaska who have helped in the search for E.T. Barnette I would like to thank John Bernet, Norma Bowkett, William Hunt, and Claus Naske.

Special thanks are also due to Ruth Allman, who gave me permission to quote from Judge Wickersham's diaries, Bob De Armond of Juneau, Cecil Robe of Eugene, and a fine editor at Alaska Northwest Publishing Company, Virginia McKinney.

I would also like to thank my father, William P. Cole, and my wife, Marjorie, to whom this book is dedicated.

Introduction

"There are a few lonely places in this world," wrote scientist and traveler Henry Elliott in 1886, "and the wastes of the great Alaskan interior are the loneliest of them all." Enclosed by mountains on three sides, the interior of Alaska was a land which few people knew well.

In the decades after the Civil War, a few explorers, adventurers and prospectors made their way into this subcontinent, which covers half a million square miles on the top of North America. Lieut. Frederick Schwatka came down the Yukon River on a log raft in 1883 and passed the mouth of a huge river known as the Tanana, the "River of the Mountains." The confluence lay almost at the geographical center of Alaska. Judging from the size of its mouth and the stories the Indians told, Schwatka thought the Tanana might be the longest unexplored river in the world.

Two years after Schwatka's expedition, the army sent out another party under the command of Lieut. Henry Allen, a young West Point graduate from Kentucky. His mission was to explore the marvelous river which Schwatka had seen. With two enlisted men and two prospectors, Allen reached the Tanana by going up the Copper River and hiking through a pass in the mountains. The party then floated down the Tanana to the Yukon.

The journey took them three months, and the five men nearly starved to death by the time they reached the nearest trading post on the Yukon, in June of 1885. The traders greeted them in disbelief. No one, to their knowledge, had ever crossed the Alaska Range to the Yukon, and they had thought it could not be done. The great mountain wall curved like a fishhook around southern Alaska, and in this range were some of the highest mountains in the world.

Despite the military expeditions and the trips made by prospectors, Interior Alaska was still largely unknown. Away from the rivers, the land held fast to its mysteries. The map Lieut. Allen drew after his expedition showed the Tanana River snaking through hundreds of miles of blank white paper.

At the turn of the century these unknown spaces attracted a man by the name of E.T. Barnette. Coming into the region as a trader, Captain Barnette stayed to build his own inland empire in the center of the wilderness. On the banks of the Chena River near its confluence with the Tanana, he founded the city of Fairbanks.

Today about 60,000 people live in the Fairbanks area. By Alaska standards the city is a metropolis. It is the largest city in the Interior and the second largest in all Alaska. Yet Fairbanks remains a man-made oasis in the wilderness. Just a few minutes off the end of the runway at Fairbanks International Airport, the land is as wild as it was in 1901, when Captain Barnette first came up the Chena River on a steamboat.

A few feet from the Cushman Street Bridge, where the main street of Fairbanks crosses the Chena, a small stone monument on the Chamber of Commerce lawn commemorates the landing of the Barnette party "near this spot." Next to Barnette's monument is a large, white milepost with arrows pointing to places such as New York, London and Paris. But Fairbanks is the city at the end of the line. The settlement E.T. Barnette founded is almost as far west as Hawaii; and on the North American continent no other community of its size is as close to the Arctic Circle. At Fairbanks the roads and the 20th century end — and the wilderness begins.

Perched as it is on the edge of civilization, Fairbanks attracts more than its share of wanderers — long-distance globe trotters who may hitchhike from Key West, Florida, or walk from Tierra del Fuego.

The founding father of Fairbanks was also a wanderer, who stayed for a time and built up a fortune and a city. Barnette started one of the most successful gold rush boom towns in Alaska. Unlike dozens of other Alaska communities that disappeared with the gold dust, Fairbanks has endured to be more than a place name on an old map.

But the history of Fairbanks and its founder is far from being only a success story.

Just 10 years after he first came up the Chena River, Captain Barnette was hounded out of the town he had founded. Disappearing into obscurity, he never returned, and his whereabouts remained a mystery. For years after he left Fairbanks for the last

Half a dozen or more sternwheelers crowd in at the Chena River dock in front of Fairbanks, 1913. (University of Alaska Archives, Charles Bunnell Collection)

time, no one could find an authentic photograph of the captain. When one picture was finally located (see page 140), there was a dispute over which person in it was Barnette. No one could remember clearly what he looked like.

Nor did anyone know where he came from, or where he died. And few people remembered the true story of how he came to be the most hated man in his own town. It all started with the discovery of gold on the Klondike and the great stampede of 1897.

For each age is a dream that is dying,
Or one that is coming to birth.

Arthur O'Shaughnessy
Ode

1

The Curse of the Cleveland

When news of the Klondike gold strike reached the outside world in 1897, it spread around the globe like a declaration of war. Overnight, the strange name "Klondike" was as well known as California. And the name summoned up a vision of Eldorado to an army of people from all over the world, people who decided that was where they had to go, no matter how far, no matter what the cost. Not since the 1840s had a strike like this been made, and no doubt this was just the beginning, because somewhere in the vast unknown spaces of Canada and Alaska, there were other Klondikes to be found.

The first two ships with the treasure from the Klondike landed at San Francisco and Seattle in July of 1897. The *Seattle Post-Intelligencer* headlined:

GOLD! GOLD! GOLD! GOLD!
68 Rich Men on
the Steamer Portland
STACKS OF YELLOW METAL![1]

The newspaper said there was a ton of gold on the *Portland*, and when the ship arrived in Seattle on July 17, dozens of men walked off the boat with their fortunes from the Klondike. William Stanley, a Seattle blacksmith, came back with $115,000

1

from his claim on Bonanza Creek. Frank Keller of Los Angeles had $35,000. William Sloat, a dry goods merchant from British Columbia, sold his claim for $52,000 in cash; and Frank Phiscator of Michigan had $96,000 in dust and nuggets lining his luggage. One man who had been a professional boxer in Tacoma was thought to be unlucky. He had only $6,000 in gold dust.[2]

Two days later a Northern Pacific Express from Seattle rolled into Helena, Montana, with 11,400 ounces of Klondike gold for the American National Bank and the assay office, gold worth about $200,000.[3] The gold was melted down and cast into five bars of 125 pounds each to be put on display in the bank windows. With the gold shipment, a letter arrived from a Helena man in the Klondike, who said that "half has not been told of the Klondike." He said that claims were being sold for anywhere from $5,000 to $750,000, with pans of dirt commonly carrying $100 worth of gold.

"The old time gold fever is beginning to manifest itself in Montana as a result of the news from the Klondike, and many are talking of departing for the north," a Helena correspondent reported in a Seattle paper. The arrival of the huge gold shipment brought crowds around the bank. "More than one old-timer who went through the stampedes in Montana in the early days feels the return of the fever. Age and hard times is all that deters many pioneers from joining the exodus to the Far North."[4]

Elbridge Truman Barnette, known to everyone as E.T. Barnette, was 34 years old and single in the summer of 1897, and perhaps he too felt "the return of the fever." Twelve days after the gold shipment reached Helena, he was on a train for Seattle, headed for the Klondike.

E.T. Barnette was born in Akron, Ohio, in about 1863. Little is known of his early life, except that according to what Barnette said later, he lived on a farm until he was 21 years old. We know that Barnette had gone west when he was in his early twenties, and had been in on several booms and gold stampedes before. But for the most part, the details are lacking. Like many of the men living on the frontier, he seemed to have no past, and wanted it that way. It was considered bad form, and could even be dangerous, to pry into the affairs of a stranger. Most men were identified by the last place they had lived, and Barnette was then known as a Helena man. It was not long before he became a Klondiker instead.

Barnette arrived in Seattle on August 2 and got a room at the

Infected with "Klondike fever," stampeders crowd aboard a vessel bound for Alaska in 1897. The only thing people are afraid of is being left behind. (University of Washington, Historical Photograph Collection)

Butler Hotel.[5] The city was crowded with stampeders bound for the Klondike. The only thing people were afraid of was being left behind.

Ten thousand people gathered on the wharf when the steamer *Portland* returned to Alaska, and after a rumor went around that the steamer *Alki* could not take everyone who had tickets, passengers waited on the dock all night long and "hugged their outfits as if they were favorite children." They were in too much of a hurry to wash themselves. Afraid they would miss the boat, they didn't dare leave the dock to get a meal.[6]

Tied up along the Schwabacher dock where the first Klondikers had walked off the *Portland* a month earlier was the steamer *Cleveland*, "as rotten a hulk as ever cleared from any port."[7] Barnette and about 160 others booked passage all the way to the Klondike with the North American Trading and Transportation

E.T. Barnette as a young man, sporting a handlebar mustache (left), and wearing his western outfit (right) sometime before he went to the Klondike in 1897. (Photos courtesy of Jeanette S. Miles)

Company. The *Cleveland* would take the eager passengers to St. Michael, Alaska, on the Bering Sea, where they could catch a sternwheeler up the Yukon River to Dawson City.

The *Cleveland* was a 32-year-old iron steamer built in England near the end of the Civil War. She had been registered under several names such as the *Scandinavian*, the *Sirius*, and the *Kahuliu*, and more than once she had almost gone to the bottom off the coast of South America. But in the three weeks since the *Portland* had docked at Seattle, every ship along the Pacific Coast not under 300 feet of water was getting ready to go north. Compared to some of the ships sailing to St. Michael or Skagway, even an unlucky bucket of rust like the *Cleveland* was a first class vessel.[8]

The gold seekers who went to Skagway had to climb through the mountains over Chilkoot Pass or White Pass, carrying a year's supply of food and equipment on their backs, and then float down the upper reaches of the Yukon River 500 miles to Dawson. The rich man's way was to take an ocean steamer to St. Michael far to the west on the Bering Sea near the mouth of the Yukon, then go by sternwheeler upriver. Compared to scaling the Chilkoot Pass or rafting the Whitehorse Rapids, taking a steamer to St. Michael was supposed to be the easy route to the Klondike.

But almost eight months would pass before Barnette or anyone else on the *Cleveland* ever saw Dawson City, and some of the passengers would never get there at all.

On the night of August 5 the *Cleveland* was loaded with 1,000 tons of cargo and 163 passengers. The dining room held only 16 people "at a rush," and most of the passengers had to sleep wherever they could find space on the deck.[9] The boat was packed as tight as a drum. But no one was turning back now because the passengers were going to be among the first stampeders to the Klondike, and they were going to be rich. For several hours the ship was held at the dock, waiting for the last mail train from the East. A reporter said it was an "impressive" sight as "the dark stole down on the crowds which waited on the dock and on the boat." In the dim light three miners with a guitar, a mandolin, and a harmonica could be seen on the forward deck of the *Cleveland* playing songs like "The Only Girl in the World for Me," "Home Sweet Home," and "She May Have Seen Better Days." One of the three musicians was singing, and "his mellow voice carried a note of sadness which seemed to affect the crowd."[10]

The reporter walking through the crowd on the dock noticed that "the reference to the maiden who had been prosperous at some preceding time was sung with much gusto and probably was connected in the minds of the singers with riches awaiting them on the Clondyke."[11] Many of them had seen better days. The harmonica player, for example, had been robbed en route to Seattle of everything he owned, and the only thing he had now was his harmonica and his ticket.

The ship cast off for Alaska at nine that night, and the spirit of the men headed north was undaunted. "As the boat drew away," the reporter wrote the next day, "there were cheers for Seattle and for everything else that could be thought of on the spur of the moment. New York had a representative aboard who yelled many

5

times, 'What's the matter with New York?' Nobody seemed to know; neither did they care."[12]

The *Cleveland* had a reputation as an unlucky ship, and on this voyage she was no luckier than usual. Ten days out of Seattle the ship almost ran aground in the fog off the Aleutian Chain, and one morning the ship's passengers and crew woke up with someone yelling "Fire!" Flames billowed out of the forward hatch, though quick work put out the fire and saved the ship. The *Cleveland* didn't sink until three years later, but the weather was so stormy in the Bering Sea that "many a time the hearts of the passengers were in their throats as the fierce gales attacked the almost helpless old tub."[13]

When the *Cleveland* anchored in the harbor at St. Michael on

With E.T. Barnette on board, the Cleveland, *"as rotten a hulk as ever cleared from any port," departs for the gold fields. In the summer of 1897, Barnette was 34 years old and single, and like thousands of others, infected with gold fever.* (University of Washington, Historical Photograph Collection)

August 18, the passengers discovered to their horror that the sternwheeler which was to have taken them up the Yukon River had left five hours earlier.

The curse of the *Cleveland* had struck, but for E.T. Barnette this was the first of a long series of accidents that would help him become one of the most powerful men in Alaska.

The scene at St. Michael was dismal. The boat scheduled to wait for the *Cleveland* had left with the passengers of another ship. The Schwabacher Dock in Seattle had seemed closer to the Klondike gold fields than St. Michael, and the gold seekers on the *Cleveland* feared they would be stranded all winter on this treeless island in the Bering Sea, a thousand miles from Dawson.

The news from the Klondike was not good either, and miners on their way from the gold fields to Seattle told frightening stories about the shortage of food in Dawson. If the reports were true, many people were going to starve before the winter was over. The returning Klondikers urged the newcomers to go back to Seattle. Years later a colorful storyteller and friend of E.T. Barnette's said, "Some of the weaker kneed sisters, with shivers running down their spines, took advantage of the opportunity of returning on the *Cleveland*, while the more hardy figured that if they could come through such an experience as had been offered them on the *Cleveland* in safety, they would be safe in the hands of the Almighty pretty near anywhere."[14]

Shortly after the little Jesuit mission steamer, the *St. Michael*, steamed into St. Michael harbor, 60 of the *Cleveland*'s stranded passengers, the hardy souls who did not want to turn back, bought the vessel for $10,500. With each stockholder paying $200, they formed a company called the Yukon Miners' Cooperative Association, the YMCA. The payment entitled each stockholder to ship about 1,000 pounds of provisions on the *St. Michael*, which a volunteer 16-man crew would bring up the Yukon before freeze-up. The men picked E.T. Barnette as captain of the *St. Michael* because he had previous steamboating experience. Two mates and an engineer also knew something about boating, but the rest of the volunteers were all novices. Among Barnette's crew members were a lawyer, a doctor, several miners and clerks, and one tramp printer.[15] Together they loaded the *St. Michael* and one barge with 35 tons of the stockholders' provisions. Then Barnette's floating circus steamed away towards the Yukon River.

On their first try, they did not make it. St. Michael is the

7

nearest deep-water port to the huge Yukon River delta; and to ascend the river, Barnette had to steam 60 miles across Norton Sound. The ocean swells rolling in from the northwest seemed to lift the boat clear out of the water, and the red paddlewheel would make two or three revolutions in the air, before the boat was almost swamped in the next swell. Captain Barnette took the *St. Michael* back to the harbor and headed into the St. Michael Canal. He waited at the mouth of the canal until nightfall, when the water was calmer, and made the run across Norton Sound in the dark, reaching the Yukon early in the morning. It took six hours for Captain Barnette to find the right channel in the maze of the 100-mile-wide Yukon delta. One of the volunteers said that if Captain Barnette and his two mates had not been "good judges of bad water," the *St. Michael*, overloaded with supplies and without a real crew, would never have made the trip successfully.[16]

Besides the continuing danger of running hard aground and getting stuck for six or 12 hours at a time, Barnette had the worry of keeping the steamer supplied with firewood. At the missions and trading posts, cordwood to fire the steamer's boilers cost $4.00 a cord. But at the small Indian camps, the Natives wanted sugar or tea instead of money, four cups for a dollar. Wherever there was no wood for sale, Barnette would send out a few men in a small rowboat to bring back long pieces of driftwood, which they could cut into furnace lengths while steaming upriver.[17]

Not everyone in Barnette's crew was interested in cutting wood. The only thing Ben Davis wanted to do was play the banjo, and when Captain Barnette invited him to "warm up on the woodpile" one day, Ben "politely declined the invitation." Barnette threatened to put him in irons, even though there were none on board. Seeing that he was not going to get any work out of Davis, Barnette finally agreed that Davis's job was to be "official entertainer."[18]

Down below, Hugh O'Donnell was the chief engineer, though as he said later, "I didn't know any more about an engine than a bull frog knows about opera."[19] Early one morning the crew almost blew up the steamboat. Barnette was in the pilot house at the wheel, when he heard the crew shouting "Fire!" He came down and found that the timbers beneath the firebox had caught fire. Immediately he ordered all doors and windows to be shut tight and blocked with sacks of flour and corn meal to cut off the drafts that might fan the flames. On either side of the river were long sandbars, and the water was too shallow to stop right away. In a desperate race against the fire in the heart of the wooden steamboat, Barnette ordered the mate to head full speed to the nearest safe landing. One mile upriver they cut the engine in quiet water and put out the fire. The *St. Michael* would have been totally destroyed, one of the crew members wrote later, "if it had not been for the coolness and rare presence of mind displayed by the captain and the fidelity in the execution of commands shown by the two mates in this hour of rare danger."[20]

One week later as the sternwheeler approached Rampart, the halfway point to Dawson, another dangerous and embarrassing accident occurred. Barnette proudly ordered the stars and stripes to be run up the flagpole. He wanted to enter the first real town they had passed on the river with the colors flying. As soon as the flag was up, however, the smoke stopped puffing out of the smokestack. In a few seconds the *St. Michael* was completely hidden by a cloud of hissing steam coming from the boiler room. The boat had lost all power and was spun around by the current for about a mile until the crew could make a landing. The cause of the power loss was a blowout in the steam pipes, and it took 20 hours to repair the damages. By the time the repairs were complete, the engine was held together with "wooden braces, ropes, and bailing wire." But the gold seekers kept on going.[21]

The little steamer *St. Michael* was just one of many intent on reaching Dawson City before freeze-up; but the riverbanks were littered with those who had given up for the year, and would winter-over at places such as Rampart. For Barnette the strain of racing the calendar with an old, worn-out mission boat — breaking down continually and run by a greenhorn crew — was taking its toll. In mid-September the captain came down with pleurisy and inflammation of his small intestines. The rocking of the boat on the water was agony to Barnette, and the doctor and the rest of the crew urged him to return to Rampart for the winter.

The weather was now so cold that water splashing on the boat froze on the rigging and machinery. Every hour or so the crew had to stop to knock off the ice. The superstructure of the boat was only a thin wooden, canvas-covered shell enclosing the boilers, and the captain's cabin was impossible to keep warm. The *St. Michael* was no place for a sick man, but Captain Barnette refused to give up. He told the men he had promised the stockholders, before he was chosen captain, that as long as any of the YMCA members were above him on the river on other boats, "nothing short of conditions which could not be overcome would keep him from taking their food to them." Barnette said he "preferred the increased chances of death aboard the boat to a failure to keep his promise."[22]

For a few days they were afraid that Captain Barnette might be the third man in their party from the *Cleveland* to die. A New Yorker named H.B. Tucker, son of the owner of the *Troy Press*, had gone out prospecting on Minook Creek at Rampart and was found frozen to death sitting upright beneath a tree. The men had no lumber for a coffin, so they buried him in a rubber blanket on the trail where he died. Another Easterner, a Syrian from Washington, D.C., had died earlier at Russian Mission.

Captain Barnette put the boat in charge of the mate and tried to rest as best he could. In a few days he was feeling better, but the chances of their getting through to Dawson City before freeze-up were getting slimmer and slimmer. They met the steamer *John J. Healy* coming downriver with 25 passengers of the *Cleveland* on board, including six YMCA stockholders. The master of the *Healy* said the season was now too late and the water too low for sternwheelers to get past Fort Yukon.

Still, the old missionary boat full of gold stampeders kept on going. At Fort Yukon the *St. Michael* picked up about a dozen stranded men and their outfits. This so overcrowded the boat that some of the newcomers had to sleep on the canvas roof. By picking its way carefully across the Yukon Flats, with men on the bow and the front of the barge regularly checking the depth of the water, the *St. Michael* reached Circle City on September 28, 1897.

Ice started running in the river that night, and most of the YMCA members decided to stay at Circle for the winter. Nineteen men, however, were still willing to gamble on getting up the river. As one of the 19 said, "We were all monomaniacs on the subject of getting to Dawson."[23] Captain Barnette was certain that the *St. Michael* would never make it; the 19 monomaniacs convinced him to try.

The ice was flowing thick and fast the morning after their arrival at Circle, and while some of the extra supplies were being unloaded, Captain Barnette sheathed the forward part of the boat with sheet iron to protect it from the ice. Then they waited 12 days for the weather to break. Finally, on October 10 the temperature went up and the river rose. Early on the morning of October 15, Barnette backed the *St. Michael* out through a channel the crew had cut in the shore ice to the open water in the center of the river. For 30 minutes he tried to go upstream, but the steamer was stuck fast, unable to breast the current.

When Captain Barnette came back to shore and landed, he announced that it was not only impossible but dangerous to try again, unless half of them would agree to stay behind and allow the others to go on. "Each man wished his neighbor to remain but wanted to go himself," commented one of the stockholders.[24] In disgust, Barnette resigned as captain. Along with his two mates, he unloaded his own supplies and baggage. Later that same day a new captain took the *St. Michael* out in the river. When he ran the steam pressure too high, the boiler started to leak again. The makeshift crew lost its wits, and the fireman shouted, "Save yourselves — the boiler is bursting." The pilot ran the boat on a bar in the middle of the river, and it took all night to get it off. The monomaniacs gave up the hopeless attempt and admitted they were "wiser men by an additional day's experience."[25]

The town where Captain Barnette and the others were stranded hundreds of miles from the Klondike had been founded only three and a half years earlier. But it had aged rapidly. In 1895 Circle City had been the "Paris of the North," the largest log cabin town in the world, with 28 saloons, eight dance halls, an opera house, a library with the complete works of Darwin, Carlyle, Irving, and Macaulay, and a copy of the *Encyclopaedia Britannica*. The main street was 60 feet wide, permitting four teams of dogs to ride into town side by side. And city lots sold for $2,000 apiece. When the Klondike was discovered, however, Circle City was abandoned. By early 1897 it had become a virtual ghost town.

For a few months at least, Barnette was going to be stranded in the old town. The captain may have sold some of his extra supplies for a good profit, because of the serious food shortage. He did have a good supply of cash, or at least enough to buy the most expensive dog team on the river, for $1,700.[26]

Barnette was always interested in good dogs and fast horses, and when he had to, he could drive his dogs like a racer. He later set a speed record with a dog sled from Dawson City to Whitehorse. With one team of dogs and no night travel, he covered the distance in six days and eight hours.[27] For the present, though, he had to wait until the ground froze solid so that winter travel could begin and he could mush on to Dawson. In the meantime Captain Barnette made the acquaintance of the new deputy Collector of Customs stationed at Circle, Charles Smith, with whom Barnette later became partners.

The gold fields to the south of Circle City were still thought to be rich, despite the mass exodus to the Klondike. So far, most of the gold discovered in Interior Alaska had been found in streams flowing north from the Tanana Hills: Circle City's Birch Creek, Fortymile Creek, Miller Creek, and others. For years the old-time miners had said that someday there would be a rich strike along the Yukon that would open up Alaska to the rest of the world. Most of the miners and those who had studied the available maps looked to the far side of the Tanana Hills as the place where the great strike would be made. This was a remote section where few people had ever gone before.

The Klondike strike in the Yukon had thrown off all those predictions. But after the Klondike discovery there were dreams of an American Klondike that would be found in Alaska, perhaps in the unknown spaces of the Tanana Valley. When the predictions of the old-time miners came true, Captain Barnette would profit more than anyone else, because he was to stumble upon the American Klondike in the middle of the wilderness.

2

The Lost Creek

Somewhere in the Tanana Hills two prospectors were lost and almost out of food. As they were trying to find their way back home, they discovered gold on the richest creek they had ever seen. Though the two men marked the creek with a cache and an overturned boat, they never found that golden stream again.[1] One of the men, Felix Pedro, was haunted for the rest of his life by the Lost Creek of 1898. On several occasions he thought he had found it, but the Lost Creek always seemed to slip away like a dream.

Felix Pedro was the Americanized name of Felice Pedroni, an Italian immigrant who never learned to write.[2] He was the youngest of six children and grew up in a small village in northern Italy, where his father mined coal. Felix worked for several years in the coal mines of Italy and France before he left Europe in 1881 at the age of 23, on a ship bound for America.

Felix didn't drink or gamble, and he worked like a mule. Years and years of shoveling dirt in someone else's mine made prospecting for gold look easy, and when the hard working drifter reached Alaska in the mid-1890s, he struck off on his own. Pedro would never be a very good manager, but he was going to be his own boss from now on.[3]

In 1898, while 30,000 people rushed to the easy pickings around

His face showing the strain of years spent mining and prospecting, Felix Pedro stares into the distance. The hard working Italian immigrant discovered, then lost, a fabulously rich gold stream in the Tanana Hills four years before a second discovery in 1902 led to the founding of Fairbanks. (University of Alaska Archives)

Dawson City, where many thought they could get rich just by showing up, Pedro discovered and lost a fabulously rich creek in the Tanana Hills. And even his friends eventually began to doubt whether it had ever existed.

For two years after his discovery, Pedro worked in the Circle City mines; and whenever he had enough supplies, he headed back into the hills. He walked hundreds of miles from the Chatanika River to the Goodpaster River, and back again, searching for the creek he had seen. In 1901 Pedro and a man named Bert Johnson crossed a ridge on two mules. While panning one of the Salcha's clearwater tributaries, Pedro found gold shining in the dirt. Thinking he had found the lost creek at last, he named the stream Ninety-Eight Creek. The water was too high at that moment to do any mining, so he and Johnson returned to Circle City to buy more supplies and tell all their friends of the discovery.[4]

A well-equipped party, the best that would ever go in search of the Lost Creek, returned with Pedro from Circle City to Ninety-Eight Creek. They staked claims on the creek and started to sink prospect holes immediately, only to find that despite good colors from top to bottom, and a few promising flakes of gold, the ground was worthless. They had spent a lot of time and used up much of their food for nothing, and most of the miners were angry with Pedro for leading them on a wild-goose chase after a phantom creek. They nicknamed Pedro the "Old Witch," and split into smaller prospecting parties, leaving Pedro alone on Ninety-Eight Creek.

Felix started out again, with another friend, probably Tom Gilmore, who came from Iowa. According to one account Pedro and Gilmore sank their first prospecting holes to bedrock on Bear Creek, the stream where they built a cage for their pet bear cub.[5] For most of the summer, however, it seems that Pedro and Gilmore worked in the mud and gravel in the Fish Creek valley. By the end of the season they were tired from the long months fighting the mosquitoes and the bears, and again they were almost out of food. To get more supplies they had to walk 165 miles to Circle City. The two of them started back on August 26, 1901.

They picked their way up the face of the wooded hill later called Pedro Dome. Pedro stopped to rest, and far across the valley he saw smoke. It could have been a forest fire or an Indian camp, but he looked with his field glasses and saw the smoke of a steamboat. This was a lucky break for Pedro and Gilmore. If the men on the steamer had any extra food to sell, the two prospectors could continue their search and save themselves a 300-mile walk to Circle City and back. Pedro watched the steamer, which was about 15 or 20 miles away, as it first tried to get through the Bates Rapids in the Tanana River, then turned back and tried to navigate up the Chena River.[6]

Pedro and Gilmore started down through the trees in hopes of flagging down the boat before it left. It took them at least a day to cover 15 miles from the top of Pedro Dome, but finally that evening or early the next morning they reached the spot on the

A photographer captures the Tanana Hills in this study of shadow and light at the turn of the century. The creeks and valleys look much the same today as they did when Felix Pedro made his big strike on Pedro Creek in 1902. (Author's Collection)

Chena River where the steamboat men were unloading boxes in a clearing in the woods.

Things were not going well for E.T. Barnette.

It had been four years since he had boarded the *Cleveland* for the Klondike. He had eventually reached Dawson City the winter

after the *St. Michael* fiasco, and for a time he had worked there as manager of some mines for the North American Trading and Transportation Company. In the summer of 1898 he had returned briefly to Montana and married an Irish Catholic woman named Isabelle Cleary, before going back to the Yukon.[7] Some investments in trading supplies and mining claims had evidently paid off. He had earned a good deal of money one winter in Circle City when supplies were low and he had a corner on the market. But that tidy profit had made Barnette more eager than before to set out on his own.

In his travels Barnette had become well acquainted with John Jerome Healy, the old Indian fighter and a fellow Montanan, who had come to Alaska in the late 1880s. Healy was the Buffalo Bill of Alaska, a hunter, prospector, trader, and big-time promoter. No man alive could make bigger plans than John Jerome Healy.

The exact nature of Barnette's dealings with Healy is not clear, but the two did correspond regarding a railroad Healy planned to build over the "All-American Route to the Klondike Gold Fields," the trail which ran 400 miles from the ice-free port of Valdez to Eagle on the Yukon River, near the Canadian border. This was the shortest route to the gold fields, and it cut through the heart of Alaska. (Healy was later one of many who proposed building a railroad across the Bering Strait to link New York and Paris. The plan fell through when he failed to get a concession from the Russian Czar.[8]) Healy's earlier scheme to build a railroad over the "All-American Route to the Klondike" was more practical, but like his railroad from New York to Paris, the line never got past the planning stage.

In conjunction with Healy's plan to run a railroad from Valdez to Eagle, Barnette decided he would establish a trading post at the Tanana Crossing, or Tanacross, the halfway point where the trail crossed the Tanana River. Healy assured Barnette that the railroad was going to be built.

"Never mind," Healy wrote Barnette that winter, "what Heney or anyone else says of the Valdez road not being built. It's going in just the same, get there without delay."[9] Barnette thought this trading post could be the beginning of the "Chicago of Alaska," a city that would open up 50,000 square miles in the Tanana Valley, with plenty of land for agriculture, excellent gold prospects, and some of the richest copper deposits in the world nearby in the Wrangell Mountains. He told the *Daily Klondike Nugget* that the Tanana Valley was "a region so vast in extent and so promising in its riches that the half cannot be told of its future."[10]

Barnette's post at Tanana Crossing would be the crossroads for the entire valley, accessible during the summer by riverboat up the Tanana River, and with year-round rail connections direct to both the Yukon and a deep-water port. Tanana Crossing may also have seemed to Healy and Barnette a natural Alaska terminus for a railroad across the mountains to Chicago and New York, and perhaps a future stop on the New York to Paris line.

To build this future metropolis, E.T. Barnette went into partnership with Charles Smith, the former Collector of Customs at

Captain Barnette's first steamer, the Arctic Boy, *ties up at a mining camp on the Yukon River. Shortly after Barnette purchased her, the* Arctic Boy *was run aground on a submerged rock and her bottom torn out. Barnette's bad luck with steamers was holding true.*

Circle City, on November 15, 1900. Barnette went to San Francisco and purchased $20,000 worth of trade goods for the post at Tanana Crossing, which were to be sent to St. Michael. He then returned to Circle City in April of 1901, where he bought a $10,000 steamboat called the *Arctic Boy*. This he piloted down the Yukon to St. Michael that spring to pick up his supplies for the new city.[11]

But Barnette's bad luck with steamboats hadn't changed. Someone on Barnette's crew was taking the *Arctic Boy* for a cruise around St. Michael harbor when the pilot ran her on a submerged rock and tore out the bottom.

The load Barnette had sitting on the dock at St. Michael weighed about 135 tons, and he now had no boat for shipping it. Barnette could salvage the machinery of the *Arctic Boy*. Other than that, it was a $10,000 piece of junk. The captain was also out of money. He had spent the entire $30,000 he had put up for the venture.

Barnette was desperate. The $20,000 load of supplies and equipment he had ordered in San Francisco was "most complete in every detail."[12] He had general supplies, one horse, a team of dogs, windows and doors, a sled, and a steam launch. In addition, he had tools, prospecting equipment, hardware, and the basic kinds of food. This was going to be only the first shipment to his Tanana Crossing trading post. Next year he planned to ship in no less than 500 tons of supplies.

Captain Barnette went to talk with Captain Charles Adams and Thomas Bruce, co-owners of the steamer *Lavelle Young*, which was then in port. Adams had seen the *Arctic Boy* go down, and when Barnette told him where he wanted to go with his large load of supplies, he thought Barnette was crazy.

"I was dumbfounded," Adams said. "Valdez-Eagle Crossing? Why, man, that's nearly 400 miles up the Tanana above Fort Weare! How are you going to get there?"

"I figured the *Lavelle Young* could make it," Barnette said. "I've talked to a couple of men about it who were supposed to know. They say we can take the steamer all the way up."[13]

Whomever Barnette had talked to was more optimistic than anyone Adams could find. All the steamboat men at St. Michael thought Barnette's plan ridiculous. The *Lavelle Young* had a draft of about three feet. Oddly enough, according to Captain Adams, she drew less when carrying a load of at least 50 tons on her bow than when empty, because the load set her on an even keel.[14] A boat the size of the *Lavelle Young* at Tanana Crossing? Impossible, the river men said. Barnette might as well take an ocean liner up the Tanana River as the *Lavelle Young*. The experts said there was no way that steamer could climb the Bates Rapids, the sandy shallows many miles long, where the Tanana is so broad it is more like a fast-moving swamp than a river.

Barnette, however, was convinced the steamer could make the

trip. Healy had told him "to get into that country, no matter what the cost," and he was not going to let the loss of the *Arctic Boy* stop him.[15] "I'll make it worth your while," Barnette told Adams. The co-owner of the *Lavelle Young* asked another captain named Patterson, who had run some logs down the Tanana, about their chances of success.

"My God, man, you can't get beyond Chena without a lot of luck," Patterson said. "That's only about halfway to the crossing! I'm glad you're trying it, instead of me."[16]

As Charles Adams wrote years later, "I then told Capt. Barnette that it was very doubtful if we could get beyond Chena Slough and after some talk we made up a contract whereby we agreed to take him to the Slough for so much a ton and if possible to take him and his outfit of 130 tons to Tanana Crossing for an additional sum per ton. It was also agreed that if we got beyond Chena Slough and could get no farther, that Barnette would get off with his goods wherever that happened to be."[17]

Adams said he was skeptical, but Barnette convinced him to make the trip. An added incentive was the $6,000 that Barnette promised to pay him, and the contract they made, which said that Adams had to go only as far as the Chena Slough. If they could get no farther, "Barnette would get off with his goods wherever that happened to be." Considering that $6,000 was more than half the price Barnette had paid for the *Arctic Boy*, it was going to be an expensive trip. But first Barnette had to get the $6,000.

With his partner Charles Smith, Barnette went to see the Collector of Customs at St. Michael, James H. Causten. The two asked Smith's fellow customs agent to endorse three notes to cover the $6,000 freight bill, which meant that if Barnette and Smith failed to pay the money, Causten would be responsible for the debt. In return they offered to take Causten in as a full partner, who would own one-third of all the mining claims and other property they staked, plus one-third of the proceeds from the sale of the $20,000 worth of trading goods. Causten agreed to sign for three $2,000 notes, one from R.H. Miller, one from E.C. Deane, and one from the owners of the *Lavelle Young*.[18]

Causten's signature on those three notes was to cost Barnette dearly five years later, and he would regret the deal for the rest of his life. But for now he had the money, and Barnette and Smith signed the contract with Causten in triplicate on August 7, 1901. Later that same day, despite the warnings of those who said the *Lavelle Young* might be wrecked if it went up the Tanana, Captain Barnette, his wife of three years, Isabelle Barnette, Charles Smith, several employees, and Captain Adams and crew steamed out of St. Michael headed for the unknown waters of the upper Tanana River.

Captain Adams said the trip up the Yukon was "uneventful," with the *Lavelle Young* stopping every afternoon about four o'clock to cut cordwood for the next day's run.[19] When the steamer turned into the mouth of the Tanana River, Adams found that the water was at a low stage, which did not bode well for Barnette's prospects. At its mouth the Tanana was "one mass of shoals and bars," and only by working the boat a foot at a time did the crew succeed in getting safely across to deeper water.[20] For a distance of 250 to 300 miles, the river was fine. Then the *Lavelle Young* reached the mouth of the Chena Slough.

The mouth of the Chena, directly below the Bates Rapids, was commonly known as the head of navigation on the Tanana. Several shallow draft steamers had previously made it up the Tanana to this point, and when the *Lavelle Young* arrived there in 1901, a small trading post was then under construction across from the mouth of the Chena.

Traders George Belt and Nathan Hendricks had contracted to build two trading posts on the Tanana River: one at Baker Creek 90 miles above the mouth of the Tanana, and another at the head of navigation near the Chena River.[21] A telegraph line was planned down the Tanana River, with a station at the mouth of the Chena, so besides getting the Indian trade and that of any future prospectors, Belt and Hendricks would supply the workers on the telegraph line.

Captain Adams had taken Barnette as far as he had guaranteed, to the mouth of the Chena, and now they continued upriver past the point of no return. Anywhere that the *Lavelle Young* got stuck from now on, Adams could drop off Barnette's goods and head back to the Yukon. The figures vary, but not far above the Chena, perhaps six or eight miles, they "came to where the river was all scattered out in a lot of channels, none of which were deep enough for us."[22] Adams did not have steam steering gear or a steam capstan on the *Lavelle Young*, so winching the boat off a shallow spot had to be done by hand. The captain tried all the channels and "backed out like a terrier searching rabbit holes."[23]

Both Barnette and Adams agreed they could get no farther this way. Captain Adams recalled what happened next. "Capt. Barnette then told me that an Indian had told him that perhaps we

The Lavelle Young, *the sternwheeler which first took Captain Barnette up the Tanana River, unloads at Fairbanks.* (Courtesy of the Fabian Carey Family)

could go up the Chena Slough and get out into the Tanana again above this bad place and go on up to the Crossing. This we decided to do, and we went back and started up the Slough. . . ."[24]

Captain Adams spun the wheel and took the 150-foot *Lavelle Young* up the narrow river the Indians called the Chena, the "Rock River."[25] About 14 or 15 miles above the mouth of the Rock River, the *Lavelle Young* again ran out of water. The deck hands tied the boat up on the riverbank about noon, and Adams called Barnette up to the pilot house, where the two of them argued for almost an hour. Neither could understand the pigheadedness of the other.

Adams said, "It's no use. I guaranteed to take you as far as the boat would go up the Tanana. I can't cross mountains with it."

"Now wait," Barnette said, "you can't put me off here, there's no place to unload. Besides, I talked to an Indian that knows a way to get through this and back to the Tanana."[26]

23

Adams had had enough of Barnette's Indian stories, and he refused to go farther. Barnette thought that at least he should get back on the main river and out of this small slough, where a shallower draft steamer would have no problem taking his supplies up to the Tanana Crossing next year. He asked Adams to take him back down to unload him at the mouth of the slough, at Belt and Hendricks's trading post.

"That's not in the contract," Adams said. "You know darn well it's downstream and we'll get stuck a dozen times. I've got to get back to St. Michael."[27] Going downstream with a full load was much more hazardous than going upstream. Traveling downstream the boat could be pushed hard and fast on a bar and the current could hold it there like a brace. Since the boat had no steam winches and the huge six-foot wheel in the pilothouse was without steam power as well, it would take hours to work the *Lavelle Young* off a sandbar. Adams could not risk any long delays so far from home, for he might get trapped for the entire winter.

Finally the two captains compromised. Captain Adams refused to take Barnette all the way back to the Tanana River, but he would bring him to a point within six or seven miles of the mouth of the slough, to a high bank with good timber they had spotted on the way up. Captain Barnette agreed to pay for any long delays. The steamer got stuck once or twice, but not seriously, and finally tied up beneath the high, wooded bank at about four o'clock in the afternoon, on August 26, 1901.[28] Later that evening or the following morning, Felix Pedro and Tom Gilmore appeared from the wilderness.

The Captain and the Judge

When Pedro and Gilmore walked into the small clearing in the woods, the sternwheeler *Lavelle Young* was tied up along the south bank of the Chena with the gangplank down. The furious E.T. Barnette was watching deck hands clear some trees and unload his freight onto the ground. The scene resembled a general store that had gone through an earthquake.[1]

But the appearance of his first two customers may have mollified Barnette somewhat. Perhaps Pedro and Gilmore fired some shots in the air to warn of their approach, as was the Indian custom. They informed Barnette that they were not the only prospectors in the area, and that maybe others would come by for supplies later in the year. The two miners were delighted at the opportunity to stock up on supplies, and they "were anxious to buy anything eatable that was for sale."[2] Pedro said he had been finding good prospects but had not yet made a strike, and he in turn listened to Barnette's sad story about his broken plan of going to Tanana Crossing, about 200 miles upriver.

Barnette, making the most of a bad situation, said he would operate a trading post from here until he could move on to Tanana Crossing. He sold winter outfits to Pedro and Gilmore, and optimistically christened the post "Chenoa City," a pretty big name for a clearing in the woods with a few tents and one unfinished cabin.[3] Felix Pedro and Tom Gilmore left with their supplies as quickly as they had come.

After the two unexpected visitors left, Adams's crew members and those who worked for Barnette constructed a small house for the captain and his wife and a big log trading post 26 feet wide by 54 feet long. By cutting the trees that were standing on the spot, they had enough logs to build the walls six feet high, and they had to go only a few feet to get the rest of the lumber they needed.[4] Tents were put up to cover most of the supplies. Two years later the first newspaper printed in Barnette's camp (on an Empire typewriter) called this group of tents and buildings "the beginning of civilization on the Tanana."[5]

It was an unusual group of people who founded this civilization, a settlement built in a day at the wrong place and at the wrong time of year. There was a man named "Shorty" Robinson; and another called "Soapy Smith the Second"; Jim Eagle, an old frontiersman from New Brunswick; Ben Atwater, who was once declared the strongest man in the United States; a Japanese cook named Jujiro Wada who was to play an infamous role in the founding of Fairbanks, and several others.[6] Barnette, the person responsible for the venture, was a man whom no one seemed to know too well.

Captain Adams was eager to leave as soon as Barnette was established. The days were getting shorter, and snow would fall within a month. Barnette had no sympathy for Adams because the way Barnette looked at things, he was in a far worse position. Stranded on the bank of a shallow stream off the main river, hundreds of miles from where he wanted to be, and with no hope of moving for at least a year, he was not pleased. Barnette gave Adams a bundle of letters to mail when he reached Dawson, but he refused to shake hands with the captain of the *Lavelle Young*. As the boat pulled away, Isabelle Barnette was crying and nearly hysterical. Mrs. Barnette always suffered from poor health, and she was not looking forward to spending a winter in the middle of Alaska.

Barnette spent that winter planning for the spring. He had sent out a letter with Captain Adams to Frank Cleary, his brother-in-law back in Montana, asking him to catch a steamship to Valdez. He sent Dan McCarty, a former deck hand on the *Lavelle Young*, south across the mountains to meet Cleary at Valdez. Not trusting anyone else with the responsibility, Barnette planned to have Cleary come in and watch the trading post, while he went outside to get more supplies and a new flat-bottomed steamer which could navigate the river to the Tanana Crossing.

Barnette traded with the Indians for some marten and fox skins, which would bring a good price in Seattle. There was talk of a gold discovery far up the Chena River on Pyne Creek, where several prospectors were wintering, but nothing came of it. It was said that Barnette himself had tried to cause a stampede that winter, but had failed.[7] Little else was going on.

Towards the end of February Dan McCarty made it back to Barnette's post with Mrs. Barnette's brother, Frank Cleary. McCarty had blazed a trail by himself across the Alaska Range up the Delta River and down the Copper River Valley into Valdez. The trip out had not been an easy 400 miles, but the return was much worse. For the last four days on the trail Cleary and McCarty had been out of food. They were caught in a blizzard and did not know where they were until the weather cleared.[8]

McCarty spent three weeks recovering from the trip. Afterwards he was rested and ready to go again, this time with Captain and Mrs. Barnette, Charles Smith, and a load of furs, over the same route to Valdez. Also traveling outside to Valdez with Barnette's party was a man named James Huntington, a mail carrier and dog musher from the lower Yukon, who had mushed into Chenoa City in the middle of winter under mysterious circumstances. Huntington said he was on his way to Valdez to catch a ship to the States. At first he started out by himself, but he returned after losing his way and waited to go out with Barnette in March.

At Rampart City on the Yukon, a story in the newspaper explained that Jim Huntington had escaped from the marshal at Tanana, and that there was a $150 reward for his arrest.[9] He had cleaned up in a poker game with some men at Fort Gibbon, the Army post at the mouth of the Tanana, and according to what he said later, the losers decided to get even with him. The losing soldiers got an old Indian "falling down drunk" on bootleg whiskey, and they told the marshal that Huntington had done it.[10] He was arrested by the marshal on a charge of selling liquor to Indians, but while Huntington was in the custody of a guard named W.J. Hamil at Frenchy's Roadhouse outside Tanana, he escaped.[11]

Huntington didn't leave the area right away, however, because the marshal arrested the guard, W.J. Hamil, and charged him with helping the prisoner escape. Back in Tanana Huntington called on his friends and businessmen in town, saying Hamil had not helped him to get away, and offered to pay the expenses to send witnesses in Hamil's behalf to his trial at Rampart.[12] Huntington, of course, had no plans to wait around for the trial. With a team of fast dogs and more than $2,000, he took off up the Tanana Valley headed for the Pacific Ocean on the other side of the mountains.

Jim Huntington, Captain and Mrs. Barnette, Charles Smith, and Dan McCarty left Barnette's camp on March 10, 1902.[13] With one man dodging the law, and everyone else feeling as if they had been locked in a frozen prison since the *Lavelle Young* had left eight months earlier, the party moved out as fast as possible on the trail to Valdez. Years later, Isabelle Pass, where the Richardson Highway climbs to an elevation of 3,310 feet to cross the towering Alaska Range, would be named to honor Mrs. Barnette for her pioneering trek that winter.

The Barnette party arrived in Valdez after almost exactly one month on the trail. The captain and his wife checked in at the St. Elias Hotel, where a reporter came to interview them. The reporter thought the Barnettes looked as if they had been on a Sunday drive through the country, instead of breaking trail for 400 miles at temperatures as low as 40 below zero. Barnette explained his plan to return to the Bates Rapids with a shallow draft steamer and run upriver, which he said "can easily be done."[14] He predicted that one day the Tanana would be very rich. He said he was going to bring in a bigger load of supplies with his new steamer to sell at Circle City prices.[15] When the steamer *Excelsior* left Valdez for Seattle about a week later, it carried the Barnettes and the others who had escaped from the post on the Chena River, except Dan McCarty, who had gone back to join Frank Cleary.[16]

Barnette, with his $20,000 stockpile of supplies sitting on a small sidestream in the center of Alaska, hundreds of miles from the nearest town, trail, or gold strike, and with only a few broke prospectors as potential customers, was eager to return as soon as possible. The furs he had brought out from the Tanana he sold for $4,000 in Seattle. Charles Smith decided he had had enough and that he wanted to get out of his partnership with Barnette. For $1,000 Barnette bought out Smith's one-third interest.[17] If Smith had not pulled out, in several years his $1,000 share would have been worth at least a million dollars, but at the time the project looked hopeless to him.

Almost all of Barnette's money was tied up in his merchandise on the Chena, and he had warned young Frank Cleary not to give anything to anybody unless there was cash up front. Somehow Barnette got another loan, and with some of his own cash he bought more supplies and a shallow draft flat-bottomed boat, which he named the *Isabelle* after his wife. Four months after he had left Valdez, Captain Barnette was back in Alaska at St. Michael, with a new boat and crew to go up the Tanana River.

The *Isabelle* had been shipped to St. Michael in pieces. In the summer of 1902 it was taking shape in the shipyard of the Northern Commercial Company under the supervision of Barnette and Matt Meehan, an old ship's carpenter from Montreal. The builders were using the old machinery and boilers taken from the wreck of the *Arctic Boy*.

One day while they were working on the *Isabelle*, Judge James Wickersham of the District Court came by to say hello. He and Captain Barnette sat down together on a piece of driftwood on the beach. Wickersham was one of the most powerful men in Alaska. He was judge of the Third Judicial District, an area covering 300,000 square miles between the Arctic Slope and the Aleutians. Wickersham's district was 10 times the size of Ireland, and for the 1,500 people who lived within its boundaries in 1900, he was almost a king. At that time there was no territorial legislature, and the Governor of Alaska had very few powers. Consequently, most of the power and prestige of the United States government was embodied in the three U.S. District Judges, who had headquarters at Juneau, Eagle, and Nome.[18]

Wickersham's stature, however, did not impress everyone. A roadhouse keeper on the upper Yukon named "Old Man" Webber, who ran one of the sloppiest roadhouses in Alaska, did not like to work any more than he had to. Webber's famous rabbit stew was said to cook all winter long in an old kerosene can above the fire, and one serving cost $2. Webber was continually adding more wild meat to the stew so he would not have to make a fresh batch until the following winter. And he did not like anyone to complain about his fare. The first time Wickersham was a guest at Webber's Roadhouse, he did not enjoy the old man's cuisine, and the judge's hunger got the best of him. He did not want to have a bowl of the "regular," and when Webber balked at cooking something special, Wickersham asked, "Man, do you know who I am?"

"Naw," Webber replied.

Built in part from the wreck of the
Arctic Boy, *the* Isabelle *lies at*
anchor on the Chena River at
Fairbanks. *Captain Barnette built*
the Isabelle *for his Fairbanks trade*
and named it in honor of his wife,
Isabelle Cleary Barnette.
(Courtesy of the Fabian Carey Family)

Isabelle Cleary Barnette
(Courtesy of Jeanette S. Miles)

"I am Judge Wickersham of the United States District Court."

"I don't give a damn, if you're Teddy Roosevelt, you won't get any better than the rest of the boys in this roadhouse!"[19]

Webber then explained how Alaska had once been a good country before the "shyster lawyers" arrived, and he was sure "it's going to hell now as fast as it can go."[20]

Wickersham was a loyal Republican from Tacoma, Washington, who as a reward for his services had been appointed judge in Alaska by President McKinley in 1900. Originally, Wickersham was to be named consul general to Japan. But after the act providing a civil code and two more judges for Alaska was passed in 1900, he became Judge James Wickersham and took off for Eagle, Alaska, instead of Tokyo.

Wickersham said he declined the post in Japan because it seemed like "hitching a very small wagon to a very distant star."[21] Maybe Tokyo was a distant star, but so was St. Michael, Alaska, on the Bering Sea, where Judge Wickersham and Captain Barnette sat talking on a piece of driftwood.

As they watched the workmen put the finishing touches on Barnette's boat, the captain talked of his plans. The two of them had met a year earlier, when the *Lavelle Young* was on its way up the Yukon. But this time Wickersham and Barnette really had a chance to talk, and the judge was impressed with Barnette. He asked the captain to name his trading post at Tanana Crossing after Senator Charles W. Fairbanks, the senior senator from Indiana. Fairbanks, a powerful figure in the Republican party who would become Vice-President in 1904, was a man whom Wickersham admired. While looking at a picture of Charles Fairbanks, Wickersham once said, "I owe to that man everything that I am."[22]

Barnette agreed to Wickersham's suggestion, and in return for the favor the judge promised to do everything in his power to help Captain Barnette succeed, which was no small promise from the most powerful government official within 300,000 square miles.[23] Barnette later explained that he and Judge Wickersham both thought the name "Fairbanks" for his trading post was a good idea. "If we should ever want aid at the national capital," Barnette said, "we would have the friendship, at least, of someone who could help us."[24] Captain Barnette knew the value of a name.

The two men shook hands on the name "Fairbanks," and the deal was the start of a long and interesting association between the captain and the judge. There would be years when the hottest

Judge James Wickersham strikes a formal pose. In later years the friendship between the judge and E.T. Barnette became a political embarrassment for Wickersham.

political issue of the day in Alaska was their friendship, and for Judge Wickersham, having Captain Barnette as a friend was sometimes the worst possible association. For E.T. Barnette, agreeing to the name "Fairbanks" turned out to be the best deal he ever made.

In August the *Isabelle* and its crew of eight men left St. Michael for the Upper Tanana River, just as the *Lavelle Young* had left the year before. This time Barnette thought he had a better idea about where he was going.

The *Isabelle* turned up the Chena River in the first week of September, and the water was so low that even this flat-bottomed vessel, especially designed with a light draft for shallow water, could not get to the spot where Barnette had unloaded his goods off the *Lavelle Young*. Four miles below Barnette's cache the *Isabelle* stuck fast on a sandbar, and Captain Barnette's skipper, Edward Thompson, told Barnette he could go no farther. Several men set out for the cache in poling boats; they were afraid that they would be stranded in the middle of nowhere for the winter, as the passengers on the *Lavelle Young* had been.[25]

Barnette's fortunes were at an all time low. After the huge sums of money he had spent on buying a new boat, it appeared that he had returned only to waste more money and another year on his "Fairbanks Trading Post." He could not even get to his cache because the Chena River was so shallow, and to remove his trading goods stored there he would perhaps have to carry them overland, which would cost more money and take more time than he could afford. Also, if the *Isabelle* could not go even as far up the Chena as the *Lavelle Young* had gone a year earlier, how would his new steamer ever be able to cross the Bates Rapids? Barnette must have felt as if he had gone to hell in a steamboat.

Then he heard the news: a month and a half before, 12 miles north of Barnette's cache, Felix Pedro had discovered gold.

4

The
Strike

Felix Pedro had spent the winter of 1901-1902 looking for the lost creek. In April of 1902 he came down out of the hills to buy another load of supplies at Barnette's cache. He was almost out of food and money. Together, he and Tom Gilmore had only $100, far too little to buy a full outfit, and unless they could get credit at Barnette's cache, Pedro would have to go back to Circle City to work for wages, and temporarily give up his search.[1]

Frank Cleary told Pedro and Gilmore that, according to Barnette's orders, he could give no credit. But Cleary, 25 years old and a former civil engineering student at a university in Montana, decided to sell Pedro and Gilmore an entire outfit — against Barnette's specific instructions. He took their $100 and "charged the balance to his own account."[2] Barnette later accused Cleary of embezzling $14,000 while he was in charge of the captain's trading post, but did nothing about it "on account of the family relationship."[3] Barnette was correct in telling Cleary that a wandering prospector was not the most reliable credit risk. But when his brother-in-law gave a load of supplies to Felix Pedro, Cleary picked the right gamble.

Felix Pedro was not a well man. It had been four years since he had discovered the Lost Creek, and the years of living in the woods had taken their toll. He was in a weak and nervous condi-

A field of tree stumps surrounds Barnette's stockaded trading post in the winter of 1903. Two years later gold had turned the rough frontier outpost into a city of saloons and three-story skyscrapers.

tion, and had a bad heart. In early July he returned briefly by himself to Barnette's cache to get more supplies from Cleary and a stock of medicine. Tom Gilmore had gone to Circle City, and Pedro was now all alone fighting mosquitoes and digging prospect holes in the frozen ground.[4]

On July 28 Pedro showed up at Barnette's store again, and Cleary must have been surprised, because he had not expected to see him for at least several months. Pedro was very excited, and he took Cleary aside to tell him that he had "STRUCK IT." He had discovered gold.[5]

Pedro said he had been working 12 miles to the north with a shovel on a small creek below the hill from which he had spotted the smoke of the steamboat 11 months earlier. No one was with

him when he made his discovery, and he never talked much publicly about the strike for the remaining eight years of his life. Pedro was too weak to dig a hole all the way to bedrock, to find out for sure how rich the creek would be. But this time he knew he had found something, and perhaps he just sat down on a rock to rest. One of Pedro's old Italian friends, "Happy Jack" Costa, later got a rich claim; and when he struck it rich, he was heard to say to himself over and over again, "Oh, by Godda, I gotta de gold!"[6] Pedro was not as excitable as Happy Jack, but he had come a long way from his village in Italy to make his way in the world — and this strike was his. He named the stream Pedro Creek, and called the hill above him, where he had first seen Barnette's steamboat, Pedro Dome.

At first Pedro told only his friends of his strike. He did not want another stampede like the last time he thought he had discovered the Lost Creek; and he wanted to make sure that if the ground was as good as it looked, he and his friends would have the best claims. In the 30 days following his strike on Pedro Creek, Pedro located four other discovery claims on four creeks in the shadow of Pedro Dome. He staked the first claims on Cleary, Gold, Twin, and Gilmore creeks.[7] Maybe he would never find the Lost Creek of 1898, but Pedro was making sure that he did not lose these.

When Captain Barnette arrived on the steamer *Isabelle* six weeks later, a small stampede was on. Barnette and all of his crew stopped what they were doing, grabbed some sardines and pilot bread, and raced off to Pedro Creek. The only people left behind to watch the steamboat were the Japanese cook, Jujiro Wada, who said he could stake no claims because he was a foreigner, and Mrs. Barnette.

Some of the men from the *Isabelle* staked on the first creek they crossed and named it Isabelle Creek, a stream that was entirely worthless. But if there was gold in the area, they were going to make sure they claimed it. Barnette had several people staking claims for him all over. He also had the power of attorney for about half a dozen relatives back in Ohio, including two brothers-in-law, two nieces, and his sister. The deal he had arranged with them was that he would use their power of attorney to stake claims in their names, and in return he would get a half interest. The claims were often staked indiscriminately. Like children on a treasure hunt, the stakers went out and claimed all the spots where they thought the prizes might be. But the gold was buried anywhere from 10 to 200 feet underground, and there were no clues to exactly where it was.

Perhaps 25 or 30 men were near Pedro Creek after Barnette arrived, and in no time at all they staked off about 110 claims on two dozen creeks. Each claim was 20 acres, marked by brush cuts and four corner posts with a location notice.[8]

On September 10, two days after Barnette's arrival, a miner's meeting was held in Felix Pedro's tent on Discovery Claim, Pedro Creek. Barnette was elected temporary recorder of the district, which meant that he would keep the books, though most of the claims were later recorded by the miners themselves at the Recorder's Office in Circle City.

Barnette had already abandoned his careful plans about moving upstream to Tanana Crossing. For two years his life's work had been to establish a large trading post where the Valdez-Eagle trail crossed the Tanana River. He dropped that scheme in an instant and decided to stay where he was: on the ground floor of a gold strike, perhaps another Klondike. Captain Barnette easily convinced the miners in Pedro's tent to approve the name of

"Fairbanks" for the town that would no doubt grow up around his log buildings on the Chena, where he had been unceremoniously dumped a year earlier.

The story of the gold rush to Fairbanks was similar in some ways to the old story about a gold stampeder named Joe Smith, who died and went to heaven. Smith walked up to the pearly gates, but St. Peter would not let him through, because he said heaven was full up of stampeders. Joe sat for a while and finally thought of a plan to get inside, so he knocked for St. Peter again.

> The Saint appeared and, nothing afeared,
>   Joe said he would like to send
> To Jack McAdoo, of Caribou,
>   A message straight from a friend.
> "Make no mistake, it's 'Jitney Jake,'
>   He's the only one you'll tell;"
> And drawing him near, hissed in his ear,
>   "There's a placer strike down in Hell!"
>
> With a glow of content, then back he went
>   To his seat on the Outer Rim.
> They were all alike, and he knew he'd hike,
>   If such a message had come to him.
> And soon they sped, with a stealthy tread,
>   Some he thought he never would see;
> They were of every date, from fifty-eight
>   To Nineteen and twenty-three.
>
> At last to the door came Peter once more,
>   And he said there was room to spare;
> But naught heeded Joe, as he muttered low:
>   "Gosh! Maybe there's something there!"
> So with eyes ablaze in an eager gaze,
>   And the look of a man possessed,
> He hoisted his pack on his old bent back,
>   And hurried off after the rest![9]

Even if E.T. Barnette or Felix Pedro were alive today, they would probably know little more about the facts behind the Fairbanks stampede than Jack McAdoo of Caribou or Joe Smith did about the stampede to hell. Barnette appears to have touched off a stampede the same way Joe Smith did, but legends about the gold rush and the way things actually happened became so confused that no one could tell the difference. Yet despite the scanty details, the broad picture is the same. Hundreds, perhaps thousands, of men rushed to the Tanana Valley.

Barnette was a true believer in blowing his own horn, and he let everyone know of his good fortune. On December 10 he wrote to his friend, Jim Morrison, a Klondiker in Seattle. "You can bet I am fixed this time," Barnette said. He explained that the pay streak on Pedro Creek was 200 feet wide and five feet deep. According to Barnette's description his trading post would become a city by the following summer. "A message came yesterday that 1,000 people had left Nome during the last three days for here. I look for half of Dawson here before spring."[10]

Things were looking better every day. Two weeks after the first letter, he wrote to Morrison again. "Our camp has improved since writing you. We have the best camp on the American side today. Pedro Creek has the most work done on it, and shows up fine. I have just returned from No. 2 Above, on Pedro. The owners wanted $2,000 of supplies, so I went over to make sure their ground was good. I found seven holes down, but not to bedrock. . . . They have already six feet of coarse gold that will average 15 cents to the pan. I found much better than that. It was the best thing I ever saw."[11]

"What I have said in this letter are facts," Barnette added, "and the man that gets here early is in it."[12]

Barnette got a little carried away with his enthusiasm. A year later the first geologist to look over the creeks near Fairbanks concluded, "Sufficient work has not yet been done to give definite information in regard to the average value and distribution of the pay dirt."[13] The prospect holes that Captain Barnette had examined at No. 2 Above Discovery on Pedro Creek (the second claim above discovery) were about 14 to 16 feet deep. The men at No. 2 Above were the Costa Brothers, Frank and Jack, two old friends of Felix Pedro's, and they were sinking four holes at a time, burning their way down through the frozen ground with open wood fires.

Using a wood fire to thaw the ground was the most primitive and slowest method. But without boilers or any other machinery, they had no choice. After the muck and tundra on the surface had been cleared away, a small fire with about one-twentieth of a cord of wood was set off with paper or a kerosene-soaked rag. When the wood was completely burned, about one foot of ground beneath the fire was thawed. This dirt was then shoveled out of the hole and another fire was built. Unless the ground was thawed, digging a prospect hole was impossible.[14]

With the wood fires, a miner could dig about a foot a day. But as the holes got deeper, it took longer because the men had to be careful not to enter the smoking shafts until the poisonous gases from the fire were dispersed in the air. To sink a six-foot-square prospect hole to bedrock, like the holes on Pedro Creek, could take weeks; and all the time the miners would have no way of knowing if there would be any gold at the bottom.

The view at No. 2 Above Pedro Creek, where the Costa brothers were sinking a total of seven prospect holes, was something like the scene once described in the Klondike by mining engineer T.A. Rickard. His depiction of Bonanza and Hunker Creeks in 1897 could just as well have been written about Pedro Creek five years later.

> In the early days of mining in the Klondike, when the frozen ground was conquered with wood fires, the 'creeks' must have looked like an inferno. If you had gone up the narrow valleys of Bonanza and Hunker during the long twilight of the arctic winter ten years ago you would have seen a picture worthy of Gustav Doré. . . . A weird silence brooded over the wastes of snow. The gloom was thickened by a pall of smoke escaping from holes in the ground, whence an occasional figure issued. Not many men were visible, for they were below in the rabbit warren of their diggings. At the top of a shaft, here and there, a weary gnome might be espied turning a windlass and emptying buckets loaded with dirt that came from a small pit beneath. The flare of red fires parting the twilight marked the beginning of the work of shaft sinking. The snow, the moss, and the fog muffled every foot-fall, deadened every sound. It looked like hell — but it was freezing.[15]

The claims on Pedro Creek may have been the best thing Captain Barnette ever saw, but he certainly underestimated the amount of work needed to put the mines into production. He told people like Jim Morrison to come as soon as possible, but the older, experienced miners who had been around were sure it would be several years before anything started to pay off. Besides spreading exaggerated reports, Barnette was also accused of salting a mine shaft with gold, and then showing it to a young army officer who was completely fooled and naturally spread the word about the rich and easy diggings in the Tanana.[16] The salting incident, however, was small potatoes compared to what happened in Dawson City several weeks later.

In the dead of winter 1903, when the days were only three hours long, and at 47 degrees below zero the foggy air was cold enough to burn the skin, a small man in a large fur parka mushed into Dawson City as if the police were on his trail. Jujiro Wada, known to most people as "Wada the Jap," was a long-distance marathon runner who had shipped aboard a whaler in 1890 from Japan, and had been a soldier of fortune for the last 12 years. In some quarters it was said that Wada had run away from a whaling ship at Icy Cape on the Arctic coast to live with the Eskimos. One story was that Wada became the "Great Medicine Man" at Icy Cape when he brought one of the Natives out of a trance, and that he used his resemblance to the Eskimos to great advantage when trading in whalebone and furs with the white man. Trouble never followed far behind Jujiro Wada, and after he enjoyed himself once too often one night with a bottle and a glass, he woke up the next morning to find that all the furs and money belonging to the Natives at Icy Cape were gone. Wada "didn't wait to write out his resignation as chief of the tribe."[17]

Wada's exploits as a dog musher were legendary. He once traveled several hundred miles from Herschel Island to Icy Cape in the middle of winter with no food. His formidable reputation as almost unbeatable in a 50-mile marathon run made him seem even faster with a team of dogs. But Wada was also a good cook, and he was the man who boiled the water and warmed up the beans for E.T. Barnette on the *Isabelle*.

Three days after Christmas in 1902 Barnette sent Wada with a packet of letters and a load of furs to sell in Dawson City. Wada dropped off the furs in Circle City and pulled into Dawson 19 days after leaving Fairbanks. The arrival of the King of England would not have received better press coverage than the arrival of Jujiro Wada from the Tanana. If Captain Barnette intended to have Wada advertise Felix Pedro's strike, the Japanese dog musher with a flair for the dramatic touch succeeded so well that he caused almost 1,000 men to head 300 miles across the wilderness in the middle of winter to the only trading post on the Chena River. For this Wada was almost hanged.

On January 17, 1903, the banner headline in the *Yukon Sun* read, "RICH STRIKE MADE IN THE TANANA," and the story was spread out across most of the front page. Wada had gone to the North American Trading and Transportation Company store, where he was met by Casey Moran, a reporter for the *Sun*. According to his editor, Stroller White, Moran was a man who regularly "demonstrated his flair for imaginative reporting." His greatest scoop had to be the story that the ruins of Noah's Ark had been found on a mountaintop in the Koyukuk. For a short

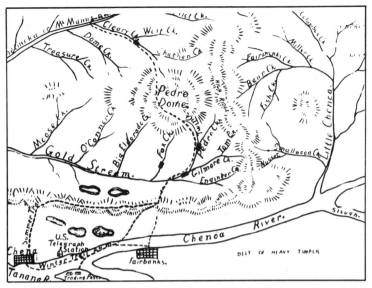

A crude map shows Fairbanks and the gold fields. Stampeders used this sketch in 1903 to guide them in their staking. (Dawson Daily News, April, 1903)

time at least the story did "considerable damage . . . to the Mount Ararat tradition."[18]

What Wada told Casey Moran was better than the one about Noah's Ark. The newspaper played up the story to its fullest. There was a crude map of the new district drawn by Wada and a large sketch of Wada himself sitting on the edge of his chair with his parka on, eagerly telling of the "wonderful riches" in the Tanana. Near the top of the page Casey wrote, "A tremendously rich strike, the magnitude of which has never been equalled since . . . the wonderful story of Klondike, has been made 18 miles north of a point on the Tanana River, 300 miles from its source."[19]

The half-dozen prospect holes in the very deep and difficult ground on Pedro Creek had become the greatest mines since the Klondike. Wada explained that the country around Barnette's trading post even looked like the Klondike, except for a "heavier growth of timber." How could a person ask for a more scientific evaluation of a mining district than that? According to the article, Wada was "known to be an unusually reliable man throughout the north." And most important, "veracity and honesty are his chief traits."[20]

43

The long distance musher was said to have read the article before it was published and vouched for every word of it.

The same claims that Barnette examined on No. 2 Above Pedro Creek owned by the Costa brothers were, according to Wada, the best prospects on the creek, with pay running 20 cents a pan. "Frank was offered $50,000 cash for his claim," Wada continued. "He would not even consider it. He figures that at the very lowest estimate he can take nearly a quarter of a million dollars out of it."[21] Wada said Pedro Creek was staked for five miles, but that there were even better prospects on Goldstream and Gilmore creeks. He listed the activity on the other creeks, giving other examples like that of No. 2 Above on Pedro Creek, and summed up by making a prediction. "Seven months from now," he said, "all the lower river boats will run up the Tanana, for surely there is a second Klondike in that country."[22]

On the day Wada's story appeared on the front page of the *Yukon Sun*, the temperature was 53 degrees below zero. Dawson was in the middle of one of the worst cold snaps of the year. A week later, not far from Dawson City at Fortymile, the temperature had gone down to 74 degrees below zero.[23] One of the other newspapers in Dawson City said that Wada's tale was a "flimsy yarn" concocted to sell copies of the *Yukon Sun,* and that any attempt to start a stampede during the coldest time of the year would be "criminal."[24]

Perhaps it was a combination of Casey Moran's eye for a news scoop and Wada's ability as a dramatist that the gold strike in the Tanana received such a favorable press in the *Yukon Sun*. The *Daily Klondike Nugget* had the story of the Tanana strike the same day the *Sun* did; but instead of plastering it across the front page, the *Nugget* ran the story as a small item on page four. The *Nugget*'s version stated, "Mr. Wada had a few nuggets with him, but spoke very modestly of the new diggings."[25] This less dramatic account also explained that everything Wada said had already been reported in the *Nugget* two weeks earlier on the visit of another man from the Tanana.

Yet it was Casey Moran's interview with Wada which everyone remembered. The story in the *Yukon Sun* started a stampede that was beyond E.T. Barnette's fondest dreams.

The
Stampede

Along the Yukon River from Rampart to Circle City and Dawson, men were on the move to the gold strikes near Fairbanks. On certain days the trails were black with stampeders pulling out with all kinds of outfits. Some went the easy way with a horse and a double-ender sled, with the passengers wrapped in heavy fur robes. Others had teams with half-a-dozen malemutes and a sled full of supplies. Many of the stampeders went the poor man's way, in harness themselves, pulling their own small sleds. They all had one thing in common. None of them knew exactly where they were going or what they'd find when they got there. Every rumor from the Tanana contradicted every other rumor. One day Pedro Creek was described as another Eldorado, and the next day it was a blank.

At a cigar store in Dawson City, the men around the stove were discussing the Tanana stampede.

"I have here a letter just received from there," a man spoke up.

The account contained a "glowing description" of the Tanana country, giving the names of the creeks where gold had been discovered, the depth of the gravel, and the richness of the pay streak.

Another man then pulled out a letter he said he had also just received. Not only was the Tanana worthless, according to this letter, but also the stampede was caused by a few men with big outfits, who wanted to unload them at steep prices.

A heated argument developed, according to a report in the *Klondike Nugget*, between those who believed in one letter and those who believed in the other, until it was learned somehow "that both letters had been written by the same individual who . . . had sprung them in that way as a practical joke just to witness the controversy that would occur."[1]

The uncertainty was characteristic of the whole stampede. There were so many contradictions it was difficult to believe anyone. Even the correct route to the goldfields was debated long and hard by people who didn't know anything about the country. Since there were no good maps and few people had much experience, some of the stampeders from Dawson City took the worst possible route. They paid for their mistake with frostbitten toes and fingers, empty stomachs, and sometimes dead pack animals. The longer but proven trail wound down the Yukon to Circle City and then south on the Tanana trail parallel to the present-day Steese Highway, where the roadhouses were evenly spaced one day's travel apart. But many Dawson men took the ill-named Goodpaster Trail, a telegraph trail that went nowhere.

Just as the stampeders were racing to Fairbanks in 1903, the United States Army Signal Corps was completing the trans-Alaska telegraph line, known as the Washington-Alaska Military Cable and Telegraph System, or W.A.M.C.A.T.S. About 2,000 miles of telegraph wire were needed to connect all the military posts in Alaska. One line ran from Fort Egbert in Eagle to Fort Liscum at Valdez. Halfway between the two a branch line was to run down the Tanana River past Fairbanks to Fort Gibbon at the mouth of the Tanana and on to Fort St. Michael near the mouth of the Yukon, then on to Nome. From Eagle a short line to Dawson City connected the Alaska system to the Canadian and thence to the United States. Later, a submarine cable hooked Alaska directly to Seattle.[2]

Lieut. William Mitchell of the Signal Corps was charged with blazing a trail to connect the completed Valdez-Eagle line with the line to go down the Tanana River and all the way to Nome. The route he chose to follow wound up a fork of the Fortymile River and down the Goodpaster River to the Tanana. Somehow the word got out that Mitchell had found an easy shortcut to the Tanana, and in January of 1903 the first stampeders started mushing over his telegraph trail to the gold fields.

Lieut. William "Billy" Mitchell, outfitted to withstand the harsh Interior Alaska winter, pauses on his snowshoes at Ft. Egbert in Eagle. Charged with building a military telegraph line, he saw the stampede to Fairbanks at first hand, and was not impressed by the men chasing after gold.

Years later when he was the champion of American air power and the "Father of the Air Force," Billy Mitchell said he had spent the long dark hours in his Signal Corps cabin on the Goodpaster River studying lighter-than-air craft and aeronautical engineering with his one-shelf library. Building the telegraph line through Alaska, he saw the stampede to Fairbanks first hand and was not impressed by the men chasing after gold on the Goodpaster Trail.

"The stampede to a new place is a terrible thing," Mitchell wrote, "especially in winter."[3]

He was glad that none of his own men deserted for the gold fields and wished that he could stop those who did not have enough supplies or the proper gear for winter travel. "People like this should not be allowed to proceed," he said, "but as this was a civil matter I had no jurisdiction over them."[4]

The United States Commissioner at Eagle, on Mitchell's advice, warned that stampeders should absolutely not go in by the Goodpaster or they could suffer "unnecessary hardship, starvation, and perhaps death."[5] Mitchell wired a Dawson newspaper directly, warning that it was the "height of folly" for stampeders to come down the Goodpaster, especially with horses, for "they are certain to meet with disaster."[6] For a distance of at least 160 miles, and perhaps farther, there was no trail at all along the Goodpaster. Nor were there any roadhouses along that stretch, and many stampeders who expected to buy supplies along the way did not know this. The Goodpaster River itself was not frozen over like a smooth highway, but was constantly overflowing and extremely treacherous. If a man with a sled hit an overflow and got soaked to the waist at 40 below zero, he would be frozen stiff in minutes.

The storekeepers at Fortymile encouraged the stampeders to take Billy Mitchell's shortcut to the Tanana because in doing so the men would buy their supplies at Fortymile instead of Circle City. Of those who took it, some got through to Fairbanks after long hardships and delays. Some stampeders spent two or three months on the trail when any other route would have taken two weeks. Many others never made it through at all and turned back after killing their dogs for food. The trail down the Goodpaster was symbolic of the entire stampede to Barnette's town. As the men on the other trails realized after they reached Fairbanks, all of them had gone on a stampede to nowhere.[7]

The mushers from Rampart and the lower Tanana River around Baker Creek reached the scene first, even before Wada had left for Dawson City. Rampart had heard of the strike from a telegram sent by Lieut. George Gibbs of the Signal Corps, who was working on the W.A.M.C.A.T. line near the Chena station. Gibbs had reportedly been fooled by a mine salted with gold by Barnette.[8] In late December of 1902 and early January of 1903, miners from Rampart were leaving every day for Fairbanks, some 250 miles away. They stampeded with the impression that $50,000 claims were open for the staking.[9] At least 150 Rampart boomers came up the Tanana River and stopped first at the trading post of George Belt and Nathan Hendricks, directly across the Tanana River from the mouth of the Chena. These men knew Hendricks and Belt, who had been trading on the Tanana River for years. The two had started their trading post below Bates Rapids at the head of navigation in 1901. They had planned to trade with any Indians or prospectors in the area and also to supply the Signal Corps during construction of the telegraph line.[10]

When Belt and Hendricks, who had been in the area longer than Barnette, said that sternwheelers would not be able to ascend the Chena River to Barnette's town of Fairbanks in the spring, the Rampart stampeders believed them. The *Lavelle Young* had had trouble on the Chena in 1901, and the *Isabelle* had made it only halfway to Fairbanks in 1902 before getting stranded on a sand-bar. If the boats loaded with supplies, machinery, and men could not get up the shallow Chena River, Barnette's town would be high and dry and would disappear when the snow did.

That spring Hendricks and Belt began to move their trading post across the Tanana River next to the mouth of the Chena, and, with the speculators from Rampart staking most of the lots, founded the town first called Tanana City and later known simply as Chena.[11] At the center of the town was the new 400-foot trading post reservation of Belt and Hendricks.[12]

Chena was much less organized than Fairbanks, where Barnette was clearly in control. Along the river Captain Barnette had staked for himself a mill site 350 feet long and 350 feet wide. After the streets were named, his trading post could be defined as the area between First and Third Avenues and Cushman and Barnette Streets. He could have reserved an entire quarter section for himself, but doing so would have chased everyone away and encouraged his customers to locate in one of the many other town sites, such as Graehl or Chena, staked along the Chena River. So Barnette took only his 350-foot square of land. Right next to his

Chena, located seven miles downriver from Fairbanks, poses a threat to Barnette's new town. But Judge Wickersham's decision to establish his court in Fairbanks, and that city's proximity to the gold fields, guaranteed that Fairbanks would prosper.
(University of Alaska Archives, Laura M. Hills Collection)

trading post, town site lots could be had in Fairbanks for the staking plus a $2.50 recording fee.[13]

The men down at Chena, on the other hand, had moved so fast that all was bedlam. Everyone wanted to have the biggest and most valuable piece of property, and the only way to stop the lot jumpers was with a rifle. Lot jumping plagued most new camps, but in Chena it was especially bad. Sometimes the lot jumpers at Chena took more than lots. Two men returned to Chena from a trip upriver to discover that everything they owned, including their cabin, had been stolen.[14]

As more stampeders arrived on the scene in the spring of 1903, the competition between Fairbanks and Chena grew increasingly bitter. Each saw the existence of the other as the single greatest threat to itself. A storekeeper in Chena was known to refuse service to anyone who lived in Fairbanks. His slogan was buy your supplies where you built your cabin.[15] Belt and Hendricks had asked Barnette to move to Chena; and Barnette, of course, had asked Belt and Hendricks to move to Fairbanks. All three traders were stubborn, however, and two major town sites developed instead of one. Chena was strictly a town of speculators and boomers founded on the first stampede. Inhabitants there did not

care about mining — until they realized that no mining was being done at all. There was no gold dust and no money in the whole camp, and their property was worthless.

No one knows for sure how many people stampeded to the Tanana in 1903. Rough estimates are that anywhere from 700 to 800 men, or perhaps a thousand or more, arrived in the spring.[16] Few knew anything about mining. A good number had left Dawson City at night, skipping out on the seven collection agencies which wanted to remind them of their debts. Saturday night between 11 o'clock and two in the morning was the best time to leave. A man with a fast dog team could make it to the American border before Monday morning and be home free, since arrest warrants could not be written at all on Sunday. One Saturday night alone, a watchful newspaper reporter counted 22 men who hit the trail for Fairbanks under the cover of darkness.[17]

Few of them found their Eldorado once they made it to Fairbanks. The creeks around Pedro's discovery were staked to the limit, and a new man could not get a piece of mining ground within miles of a discovery claim.[18] Yet almost no mining was being done on the hundreds and hundreds of claims staked in the area, most of which were staked and located with power of attorney by a few groups of men for themselves and their friends. A single man was reported to have 144 claims of 20 acres each. This meant that one man alone had tied up almost 3,000 acres of mining ground.[19]

A pencil miner like that had no desire to go down in a hole in the ground to dig for treasure. He was interested only in speculation; he did not care about getting in a supply of firewood or building a cabin on a claim. He wanted to sit back and let the money roll in and leave the hard work to the people who were not able to stake their own ground. Since power of attorney claims had strangled the creeks, not enough mining had been done around Fairbanks to justify a stampede to the corner bar, let alone a rush of 1,000 men 300 miles across Alaska in the middle of winter.

This grim truth was finally brought back to Dawson City on March 30, 1903, by a man named James Monroe, known to everyone as Curley, or Coatless Curley Monroe. Curley was a respected mining operator who was hired by a party of Dawson businessmen to go to the Tanana and once and for all bring back a straight story as to the actual conditions. Contradicting accounts were still coming back to Dawson every week, and each informant was said by the newspaper which interviewed him to be "thoroughly reliable and a conservative mining man, not given to exaggeration." The "Truth of Tanana" changed drastically every time a "thoroughly reliable" miner returned from there, and Curley's job was to get the low-down truth about the strike.

Coatless Curley never wore a coat. No matter how cold it got, he would walk around town wearing only a vest and shirt; but it was said by those who claimed to know that he always wore three suits of heavy underwear.[20]

Curley Monroe and his traveling partner, D.E. Griffith, left Dawson with a great deal of fanfare on February 27. One of the newspapers predicted that Curley would leave Dawson without wearing a coat but that inside his sled he would probably stash "an overcoat or parkey, mitts and other paraphernalia found so handy on the trail."[21]

Two days later the newspaper received two telegrams from Fortymile reporting Curley's progress. The first was not signed but was undoubtedly from Curley himself. The telegram read: "Curley Monroe reached here at 8. No hat or shirt. Very warm."

The second telegram, from a roadhouse operator at Fortymile, gave a different account of the arrival of the "shirtwaist sage."

Dud McKinney wired Dawson: "When Curley reached here he wore caribou coat and mitts. Doffed them just before entering town. Evidence a cinch. Tell all the boys."[22]

With or without a coat, Curley Monroe was a respected old-timer and well-to-do mining man. He was not a rumor monger and could not be fooled by a lot of nonsense. Some people would believe anything as long as you mentioned the word "gold," but Curley knew the work that went into a successful claim. Many who were thinking about taking off for the Tanana decided to wait until Monroe returned with his report.

Exactly one month after he left, Curley was back in Dawson City. He brought back his $10,000 bank roll intact because, he said, too little prospecting had been done to gamble on purchasing either mining ground or town property. Curley said that the Tanana old-timers on the creeks near Fairbanks were asking people they had known in Dawson: "What are all you damn fools coming into this country at this time for anyhow?"[23] Perhaps in six months or two years the Tanana might be a worthwhile camp, but as yet there was absolutely no justification for a stampede.

Curley declared that the only money in circulation was what the stampeders had brought in with them and that a working man could make no wages because no one had any money with which to pay him. A man couldn't even sell a $20 piece of gold for $5 cash money, let alone find a paying job.[24]

The stampeders stuck in the Tanana were in a terrible situation. Many had spent all they had on getting there and now had no money, no supplies, no jobs, and no way to leave until after spring breakup. "They have been flim flammed," a Rampart newspaper said, "and their only chance for getting their money back is a rush of 'live ones' from Dawson and Nome." The live ones, however, had stopped coming. The stampeders had been "cruelly faked and hoaxed," and, the editor concluded, "the instigators of such fake propositions should be prosecuted."[25]

The boomers in Fairbanks were thinking of more than just prosecution. They wanted a hanging, and Jujiro Wada, or even E.T. Barnette, was the man they would have liked to string up. There are conflicting accounts of the misfortunes of Wada and Barnette. After his pilgrimage to Dawson in January, Wada had returned with 150 pairs of socks, which he was selling for $1.50 a pair. But his position as a small businessman did nothing for his reputation.[26] There was a serious food shortage in the Tanana, and this made everyone a little desperate.

"The boys are not living on fancy meals in any part of the camp," one man said that spring. "If it comes to the worst, the 3,000 or more dogs and the several horses will not make bad steaks."[27] At a miners' meeting held to discuss the food shortage, no one liked the idea of dog or horse steak, so the men decided that they should punish Barnette and Wada, whom they saw as the cause of all their troubles. The miners suspected that Barnette was hoarding supplies, waiting for the prices to go even higher. The irate miners voted to force Barnette to sell his food immediately.

At a mock trial, Wada was forced to explain the story he had told in the *Yukon Sun* on January 17, 1903. Wada claimed that he had described conditions as they were when he had left. According to Wada, the more digging that was done, the less gold was uncovered. It is not clear how close Wada actually came to having his neck stretched by the angry miners in Fairbanks, but they certainly did succeed in terrifying him.[28]

The miners' meeting fingered Barnette as the real instigator of the phoney stampede. He was the one who had invented Wada's fairy tales and had planned the stampede to make the most money selling his supplies. They thought his prices were too high, at $12 for a sack of flour, and they disliked his policy of refusing to sell flour alone. Each customer who bought a bag of flour also had to purchase at least three cases of Barnette's canned goods such as tomatoes and potatoes, which the miners claimed were spoiled. Barnette explained that he was only trying to divide his supplies as evenly as possible. The miners voted to march down Front Street with a "nicely noosed rope" looking for Captain Barnette. With a show of force, they planned to make Barnette dispose of his flour immediately and, if necessary, take over his trading post. Barnette learned of their plan and posted 12 men inside his store, each armed with a 30-30 rifle.[29]

Before there was any bloodshed, the miners' group and Barnette came to an agreement. The captain agreed to cut the price of his flour in half and also stop forcing the miners to buy canned goods with their flour. Anyone who had the money could buy as much flour as he wished. In three days Barnette had sold out of flour. But the miners were still suspicious. They believed that one reason his shelves were empty was that he had secretly sold large amounts of flour to his friends while the miners' meeting was going on, and that somewhere he was still hoarding more.[30]

Barnette's reputation as a trader was not a very good one. No one ever accused him of being too liberal or easy with credit. The fact that he had to fortify his store like an army outpost and even build a wall around it did not say much for his skill at customer relations. He ran his trading post like a ship, and he was always Captain Barnette, the man who gave the orders.

Soon after the battle over Barnette's flour, he and Mrs. Barnette left quietly for Dawson with his "crack" dog team. When he arrived in Dawson several weeks later, Captain Barnette was interviewed by all the newspapers in town. He gave reporters a map of the Tanana diggings, and he told them he was going out for supplies and hoped to be back to take the first boat to Fairbanks in the spring.

"No, I do not anticipate very much of a cleanup this year," said Barnette, in a monumental understatement. "The claims owners are all persons of limited means and their time will be devoted more to prospecting their claims than to the taking out of a dump."[31]

Barnette joked with a reporter, making an amusing tale of the way the miners' meeting scared Wada; and the captain gave his own version of the dispute over selling his flour.

"I had quite a quantity of grub in stock and was for dealing it out a little at a time in order to prevent any possible corner, and to make it reach as far as possible, I would sell but one sack of flour at a time. And as I had three tons I could have made it go quite a ways. The people finally became so clamorous that to avoid being constantly importuned I decided to sell anything I had that might be wanted, and in a few days my shelves were swept clean."[32] Before agreeing to sell, Barnette described how he had posted a dozen riflemen inside his store. If "the so called miners meeting" had raided my trading post, Barnette said, "they would have had the warmest reception some of them had ever experienced."[33]

Barnette also described jokingly the scene on the trail from Fairbanks, when Mrs. Barnette had seen another woman for the first time in eight months. They stopped to exchange greetings, and the captain exclaimed, "you should have heard those women talk."[34] On the trip south he would attend to business in Seattle and San Francisco, he told the newspapers, while Mrs. Barnette had a nice, long vacation in civilization.

While Barnette was on his way to California, Judge Wickersham was headed to Fairbanks. The two had met briefly at Circle

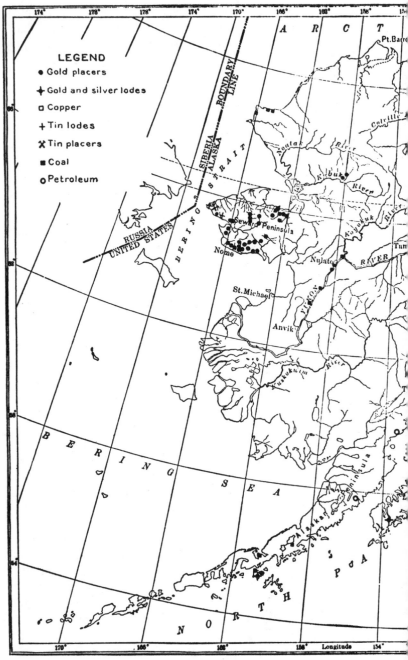

A 1904 map shows the mineral deposits of Alaska "so far as known," and the leading gold rush towns.

(U.S. Geological Survey)

City, where Barnette told him of the conditions in the Tanana. The judge had already learned that there was a great deal of crime and lawlessness in Fairbanks and had decided to go to the town he had named instead of beginning his scheduled trip to the Koyukuk.[35]

With a fully loaded sled pulled by six big Indian malemute dogs, the traveling judge stopped on the far bank of the Chena River several weeks later to have his first long look at Fairbanks. "A rough log structure with spread-eagle wings looked like a disreputable pig sty," Wickersham wrote, "but was in fact, Barnette's trading post, the only mercantile establishment in the new camp."[36] At the heart of the entertainment district were a half-finished, two-story log cabin without doors or windows called the Fairbanks Hotel and two small log cabin saloons. Barnette had a small log house for himself and Mrs. Barnette, and a stable for his horse.[37] Wickersham described the panoramic view from across the river. "A half-dozen new squat log structures, a few tents . . . a small clearing in the primeval forest — that was Fairbanks as I first saw it on April 9, 1903."[38]

Wickersham stayed in a small room off Barnette's store furnished for him by Frank Cleary, Barnette's brother-in-law. The first thing he did after a good night's rest was to ask Cleary to name the two main streets Cushman and Lacey after two members of the United States Congress, Francis Cushman from Tacoma, Washington, and John F. Lacey of Iowa. This was promptly done. The judge had now enshrined the names of two more politicians besides Senator Fairbanks in Barnette's town.[39]

The judge and the captain could not have cooperated more fully had they been business partners. Cleary had been instructed by Barnette to give Wickersham the southeast corner of his trading post at Third and Cushman to build a jail and perhaps even a courthouse. For Wickersham's own personal use, he also deeded the judge a smaller, 49-foot lot on the northeast corner of the trading post at the intersection of First and Cushman. This lot was one of the choicest in Fairbanks and soon had a market value of $1,500 to $2,000.[40] Years later, in a debate on Wickersham's reconfirmation by the U.S. Senate Judiciary Committee, the gift of this lot would be brought as evidence against the judge by those who alleged that he had been bribed by Barnette. Later a saloon was built on the lot, which made Wickersham a good sum.[41]

Soon after the judge arrived in Fairbanks, he was asked by the people of Chena to look over their town site and locate the government facilities at the mouth of the river. The judge spent an entire day examining the town of Chena. He was treated to a fine dinner at Hendricks's trading post and was shown around town by a committee of leading citizens. Wickersham saw about a dozen completed buildings at Chena and maybe 100 more under construction. That night Wickersham wrote in his diary that Chena was as busy as Fairbanks and had the advantage of being on the main river, but that he had decided that he would build the jail and locate the government offices in Fairbanks.

There was probably never any doubt in Wickersham's mind about locating the government offices in the town he had named, but his decision to go ahead and start construction of the little log jail with three cells at the corner of Third and Cushman put the official seal of approval on Barnette's town. Provisions were still short, and the boomers had gone sour on the country, but Fairbanks was growing every day. Three streets were blazed through the woods parallel to the river: First, Second, and Third Avenues. A winding path of dirty black snow a few feet wide led down Second Avenue. On either side of the path were stumps which had not yet been pulled, and big piles of spruce logs that men had chopped down to clear the streets and build their cabins.

Wickersham estimated that 500 people were living in Fairbanks, and that most of them were living under canvas, building their cabins like second skins around the outside of their tents. Sawdust and whipsawed logs were everywhere, and more buildings were going up all the time. One count put 1,000 people in Fairbanks, with 387 houses either finished or in the process of construction, six saloons, and no churches. There was also a newspaper, *The Fairbanks Miner*, which at $5 a copy was perhaps the most expensive newspaper in the world.

Judge Wickersham and several others who were short on money were planning to climb Mt. McKinley, and they published the *Fairbanks Miner* to raise some cash. The editorial policy of the *Fairbanks Miner* was straightforward: "Published occasionally at Fairbanks, Alaska, by a stampeder who is waiting for the snow to melt and the ice to go out of the rivers. . . . If you don't like our style, fly your kite and produce your 30-30."[42] Wickersham wrote every word on all eight pages of the paper, except for a long poem in the middle. A public stenographer named G. Carlton Woodward, who had brought a small Empire green-ribboned typewriter with him from Dawson, typed the entire issue. They made seven copies of the paper. Three were put up in the saloons and one was mailed to Senator Fairbanks. Only one issue of the *Fairbanks Miner* was published because the ice went out just as they were going to press.

For days before the ice went, the boomers had been sitting on the banks of the Chena, whittling. When a man started whittling, the old-timers used to say, he was soon going to hit the trail. After the ice broke, the impatient and hungry men went downriver in small boats, hoping to catch an early steamer to Dawson. Not until the middle of the summer, however, did the first steamer with a load of passengers directly from the Tanana reach Dawson. What had the 64 men and women on the boat from the Tanana found there?

"Hot air and townsite boomers," Alex Prudhomme said. He added that the Tanana was a "dead one" from the beginning.

"Ham Grease Jimmie" said the Tanana was so bad it could not support one dance hall, and he claimed that all the other gamblers had pulled out for Nome.

Carrie Lowe, a "laundress, clairvoyant, mind reader and fortune teller," was also interviewed by the press as she got off the boat in Dawson.

"How is Tanana?" a reporter asked Mrs. Lowe.

" 'On de bum,' responded Carrie in a voice that could be heard across a Manitoba wheat field."[43]

Judge Wickersham did not think the fact that the Tanana could not yet support one dance hall was the end of the world. The judge shared the conviction of a small but dedicated group who were convinced that the Tanana was going to be a steady, low-grade camp. The gold was deeper underground here than in the Klondike, and for men to sink prospect holes and mining shafts for drift mining, machinery was a necessity. For the present the bottom had fallen out of the stampede, and in June, 1903, good cabins on city lots were unloaded by departing boomers for as little as $10.[44]

For all the hardship and suffering that the stampede had caused, it did speed up the time-consuming and backbreaking work of prospecting the creeks. Preliminary work that would have taken years if done by a handful of men was accomplished in months by the hundreds of prospectors who had nothing else to do. This intensive prospecting paid off within six months when miners made three major discoveries on three different creeks — and started a second stampede that would make E.T. Barnette a millionaire.

6

The Mayor of Fairbanks

In the spring of 1903, Captain and Mrs. Barnette were staying at the Palace Hotel in San Francisco, the huge 800-room luxury inn that was known as "the world's grandest hotel." It was the finest symbol in the West of what a gold rush town could become. On their arrival, a reporter from the *San Francisco Examiner* had interviewed Barnette about his adventures in Alaska; and with the publicity from the interview, there was a "constant stream" of people coming by their hotel room asking about the gold fields. Barnette was so busy talking to visitors that it was almost impossible for him to do business, but the captain would not have wanted to come to San Francisco any other way. He told anyone who would listen that as soon as the rivers opened, there was going to be a big rush to the Tanana.[1]

Barnette had come to California to negotiate with the Northern Commercial Company, the big Alaska trading firm headquartered in San Francisco, about the purchase of an interest in his trading post. The Northern Commercial Company had already received a rather favorable report on the Tanana diggings from Charles McInroy, the NC agent at Circle City, and the company announced to the *Examiner* that it would vouch for anything Barnette had to say.

McInroy had gone into the Tanana back in February to investigate the new district and then wrote a long report, which was sent to all Northern Commercial agents in Alaska and to the home office in San Francisco. He had written that the people of Chena were making a strong play for their town, but he thought Fairbanks was the better location.

McInroy reported carefully what Barnette had told him. "Mr. Barnette . . . states that he is perfectly easy in his mind, as he is certain that the opening of navigation will establish that Fairbanks is the natural townsite for the district and at the head of good navigation."[2] Barnette had told McInroy that he had kept careful statistics the preceding summer, which he claimed was a "record season for low water," and that as late as September there was a depth of five to six feet of good water all the way to Fairbanks. Captain Barnette's statistics and his assertion that 1902 was a "record season for low water" were both highly suspect: his post had been on the Chena for only one summer. McInroy informed his superiors in San Francisco that even if Barnette was wrong and the Chena was not a navigable stream, the town of Chena was still too far from the mines. He thought a far better town site than the so-called "head of navigation" could be located directly south of Fairbanks on the Tanana River.

With his arguments about the wealth of the mines in the Tanana, Barnette convinced the Northern Commercial Company to become his partner at Fairbanks. The company bought a two-thirds share of his trading post, no doubt for a good sum. Now that he had the jail, the government offices, and a branch of the Northern Commercial Company, all of which would attract more people to Fairbanks, he arranged to have the first post office in the Tanana located in his town as well. The first postmaster of Fairbanks was Elbridge Truman Barnette, commissioned in Seattle on May 4, 1903, with the Fairbanks Post Office scheduled to receive mail 12 times a year by riverboat.[3]

After taking care of business with the NC Company and getting himself appointed postmaster of Fairbanks, Captain Barnette arrived back in Dawson City in time to take the first boat of the summer to the Tanana. With him on the sternwheeler *Seattle No. 3* were several men from the Northern Commercial Company, including Howard Turner, who was to help manage Fairbanks's Barnette-Northern Commercial Company store, and Captain Hibbard, the company's master of transportation. Also loaded on the *Seattle No. 3* were 75 tons of freight to stock the new branch store.[4]

The trip was a dismal beginning to Barnette's partnership with Northern Commercial and a bitter disappointment. As one of the Dawson newspapers reported, "Easily 2,000 people were thinking last winter of leaving for the Tanana 'on the first boat' this summer. The number dwindled to half a dozen, for no more than that started for the diggings on the *Seattle No. 3* last night. The bottom has dropped out of the Tanana boom. . . ."[5] Three of the six people on their way to the Tanana were Captain Barnette, Howard Turner, and Captain Hibbard. After all of Barnette's big talk in San Francisco, the rush to the Tanana had turned out to be a six-man stampede.

The entire summer of 1903 was as disappointing as the six-man stampede in May, especially for Captain Barnette and the Northern Commercial Company officials. Other creeks were prospected and staked, including Elliott, Miller, Vault, O'Connor, and Little Eldorado, but everyone had to scramble to exist. By chopping wood, picking berries, and hunting and fishing, the 300 to 400 miners in the area scraped together enough money and food to survive. "Two Step" Louie Schmidt had brought in eight ounces of gold dust early in the summer, which he had rocked out of a drift on Goldstream. This was the first real poke of gold ever produced in the camp, and it inspired everyone to keep working and hoping.[6]

The big strike came later in the fall. On No. 8 Above Fairbanks Creek in easy-to-work, shallow ground, where bedrock was only 10 feet below the surface, Dennis O'Shea "struck it rich." His claim was one of the richest ever discovered in Fairbanks. On occasion he got as much as $136 worth of gold in one pan.[7] Before the discovery on No. 8 Above was made public, Harry Badger walked out to the claim with his friend Bob McChesney. When they asked, "How's it going?" a man on the claim replied, "None of your business." Badger said he was curious about what was going on, so he sneaked back to the dump and took a bandana full of dirt. This handful of dirt had $2.50 worth of gold in it, a good sum when an average daily wage was $5.

Several days later Badger heard of a good claim on Cleary Creek, which he also examined. The man on Cleary was proud to say that he had found a streak of gold from the top to the bottom of his drift. These two discoveries were enough for Harry Badger. He went back into town and opened a real estate business in Fairbanks because he said he knew the town was going to be booming as soon as the news got out.[8]

After the men dig out the paydirt underground and haul it to the surface, the miners run it through sluice boxes to wash out the gold.

64

A rugged looking crew on Cleary Creek eyes the photographer before riding down to the bottom of the mine shaft in a bucket attached to a steam hoist. (University of Alaska Archives, Margaret Lentz Collection)

On Discovery Claim on Cleary Creek, Jesse Noble had been finding pay all summer. At first people called him a liar when he described the pay dirt at the bottom of his shaft, so Noble started telling everyone he wasn't finding anything, which satisfied his questioners.[9] Not much prospecting work had yet been done on Cleary Creek, which later turned out to be by far the richest stream in the Fairbanks district, and perhaps in all of Alaska.[10] The depth to bedrock on Cleary varied from 14 to 80 feet, but the average hole was about 50 feet deep.[11] Noble had one of the few boilers in the whole district, a small six-horsepower boiler fired by cord wood with five steam points. With his "tea kettle boiler" Noble had seven men working on Discovery Claim all summer, and he reported that his cleanup in the fall "was much in excess of expectations."[12]

About the same time that Noble was drifting down with his boiler on Cleary Creek, a man named John Mahilcik was prospecting Ester

Creek. In November of 1903 Mahilcik made a strike on that creek, but for eight months his discovery remained a secret. Mahilcik could not read or write. He had no way of letting his partner — Deputy Marshal George Dreibelbis at Rampart — know of the strike without telling someone else. Mahilcik did not want to leave the ground and didn't trust anyone to write out the news and keep the secret, so he simply passed the word along with those going down to Rampart that he wished to see Dreibelbis as soon as possible. The deputy marshal, who had grubstaked Mahilcik, did not drop everything and run when he received the message; but when he came to Fairbanks eight months later, Dreibelbis learned that thanks to his loyal friend he had a share in a creek that would be second only to Cleary.[13]

These three creeks, Cleary, Ester, and Fairbanks and their tributaries, were the streams that made the millionaires, as Bonanza and Eldorado Creeks had done in the Klondike. Almost two-thirds of the gold mined in the Tanana before 1910 came from the big three, for a total of more than $30 million.[14]

The gold on Cleary Creek, however, was far deeper than the gold on Eldorado had been in the Klondike. Some of the deepest shafts would have to go down as far as 200 feet below the surface, with the digging alone costing up to $10 a foot.[15] Not everyone could afford to dig a $2,000 hole in the ground, which was just the beginning of the costs. A steam hoist was needed to haul both dirt and men from bedrock to the surface. With the boilers burning cords of wood on topside, the men down below would hammer steam points into the frozen ground, or if the hot-water method was used to thaw the dirt, the miners wielded cotton hoses with firemen's nozzles shooting streams of hot water at the ground to be thawed.

The hot-water method was preferable in the Tanana because it would melt only the ground which a miner wished to melt and leave the dirt above his head solidly frozen, with timbers spaced every six feet. The steam method would often leak steam into the air, heating up the drift and making visibility poor. There was also the danger that the steam would melt the roof and cave in the whole excavation.[16]

From the bottom of the mine shaft a long tunnel was dug six feet high and six feet wide running 25 to 50 feet in each direction along the pay streak. Every foot of dirt had to be thawed, dug out, and hauled to the surface. This underground cave, averaging 50 to 100 feet in length, ran through the center of the gold-bearing dirt. Once the main runway was completed and board planks were laid to make a gangway for the wheelbarrows, the miners started cross-cutting small drifts, or caves, off the main tunnel to uncover more of the pay streak. A diagram of the mine would look like the top of a crowded telephone pole, with half a dozen cross-cuts at right angles to the main tunnel.

A typical drift mine on Cleary Creek, once adequate machinery had been brought in to thaw and remove the dirt, was No. 11 Below Discovery, which had a seven-foot square shaft running 70 feet down to bedrock. Mining engineer T.A. Rickard described his visit to No. 8 Below on Cleary in his book, *Through the Yukon and Alaska:*

"We went underground," Rickard wrote, "standing erect on the edge of the bucket and holding the steel rope, while being quickly lowered to the bottom of the shaft."[17] Rickard and his companions were given candles by the manager of the mine and walked along the boardwalk, stepping aside to let a procession of six men pass with wheelbarrows, each wheelbarrow loaded with 375 pounds of gravel. These men hauled the dirt to the hoist at the bottom of the shaft and then headed back down the tunnel for another load. The main gangway on No. 11 Below was 200 feet, and some of the crosscut drifts stretched out from 240 to 300 feet.

Even with the best thawing and hoisting equipment available, a tremendous amount of manual labor needed to be done at the bottom of the mine. On the bigger claims miners carved out virtual underground cities by hand and hauled all the dirt up to the surface, then washed out the gold. The men who dug the tunnels and moved the dirt were paid $5 a day plus board.[18] As long as the drift was cold enough, the work was hard but relatively safe, especially if the men were careful to stay away from any overhanging loose gravel.

The gold was deep in the ground, especially on Cleary, Fairbanks and Ester creeks. And the stampeders on Wada's trail had not recognized the true nature of the wealth of the Tanana mines. But by the fall of 1903 the miners could tell the good ground from the bad, and there was no longer any doubt that the Fairbanks mining district would be one of the richest ever discovered in Alaska. The work went slowly, however. Besides a few small boilers like the one Jesse Noble had on Discovery Claim on Cleary Creek, no one had the proper machinery. Using wood fires to sink the shafts and hand-cranked wooden hoists to bring the dirt up out of the ground, the miners worked on through the winter.[19]

A crew of the Union Mining Company works at the face of a placer mine deep underground in the Fairbanks district. For $5 a day stampeders who hadn't been able to stake their own claims worked the mines, carving out virtual underground cities. (University of Alaska Archives, Archie Lewis Collection)

This time there was no real stampede to the Tanana, but the number of miners increased gradually. From Dawson, Nome, Valdez, and Seattle, they came in over the trails. By Christmas of 1903 there were between 1,500 and 1,800 mining men in the Tanana — far more than the total number that had participated in the Wada stampede. Few of these miners were town site boomers or mere speculators. For the most part they were working men who spent their time either cranking a windlass or shoveling dirt into a bucket down at the bottom of a shaft.

The lack of machinery was far from being the most serious problem the miners had to face. According to one report, there was an extreme shortage of food, clothing, and all other supplies except for sugar, hardware, and whiskey. Again everyone else's misfortune turned out to be Barnette's fortune. Back in May when Captain Barnette and the Northern Commercial Company had shipped in 75 tons of supplies, hardly anyone else had brought in any food at all. Most traders had been convinced that the Tanana was a bust. So for the second year in a row Barnette had a virtual monopoly on trading goods in Fairbanks.

Normally the trading posts in the north might start to run out of certain supplies at the end of the winter, but that fall before a chill filled the air or snow lay on the ground, the Barnette-Northern Commercial Store food stocks were almost entirely depleted. In September, just as the mining ground began looking better and better, the food available for sale in the Tanana Valley ran out. In one of the first issues of the tabloid *Fairbanks News*, a newspaper founded in September, 1903, the Northern Commercial Company published an announcement which read:

That part of the resident public who are looking to this company
for their winter supplies, are hereby warned
that we are entirely sold out of
Flour
Bacon
Rice
Ham and Potatoes.
There still remains a very limited supply of
Rolled Oats
Corn Meal
Beans
Sugar
Cream and Milk
Canned Goods
Dried Fruits
Canned Fruits and
Canned Meats.

Northern Commercial Co.[20]

To assure the residents of Fairbanks that the shortage was real and not just a scheme of Barnette's to drive up prices, Judge Wickersham's brother, Edgar Wickersham, whom the judge had appointed deputy marshal of Fairbanks, was called in to vouch for the truth of the announcement. Over the signature of "Edgar Wickersham, Deputy U.S. Marshal, Fairbanks, Alaska," it stated, "I have examined the stock of the Northern Commercial Company and verified the above statement. All persons who are with-

When all the work is done at the end of the clean-up, the miners add up their take. (University of Washington, Historical Photograph Collection)

out provisions for the winter, would do well to make their arrangements before the last boat leaves."[21]

That was easy enough for a well fed man to say, but the last boat could be leaving any day, depending on the weather. The possibility of starving to death suddenly became real for the first time to many of the men in Fairbanks and on the creeks. Few people had known how little food there was on hand, though Barnette admitted he and Howard Turner had warned many of their friends weeks earlier.[22]

A string of log cabins along a rugged waterfront marks Fairbanks in 1904. (University of Alaska Archives, Robert Jones Collection)

Immediately following the official announcement, the scene at the Barnette-Northern Commercial store was bedlam. The panic of the mob swept away everything in its path. To those who had been in Dawson in the fall of 1897, the struggle for food was something they had been through before. During that first big year in the Klondike, all the money in the world could not buy a bag of flour. Before the Yukon froze that year a panic-stricken trader ran through the streets of Dawson yelling like a mad man "Run for your lives," for there was no food for the winter.[23]

The Northern Commercial store put the rest of its supplies on strict rationing. Each person could purchase only two 10-pound sacks of corn meal or rolled oats, which were the staples since no flour was left. In less than a week all the corn meal and most of the rolled oats were gone.[24]

Though it was going to be a winter of hunger for many people, Fairbanks was now boasting that it was the "largest log cabin town in the world today, and the number of buildings will be doubled by the first of the year."[25] Ten years earlier the "Paris of the North" had been Circle City, but now it was Fairbanks.

On November 1 a proud resident of Fairbanks wrote that there were 500 houses and 1,200 people in the city. But that was not all. Thanks to Judge Wickersham, the offices of the federal officials, commissioner, marshal, clerk of the court, and recorder were all in Fairbanks. The proud resident also named all of the businesses in Fairbanks. At the top of his list was written, "seven saloons," and the list continued:

two stores	one jewelry store	two meat markets
two cigar stores	two tin shops	two dry stores
four hotels	one machinery depot	one hospital
one newspaper	three large sawmills	two laundries
two barber shops	four lawyers	two bath houses
one blacksmith shop	four doctors	two carpenter shops

He noted that there were also two bakeries, "which have gone out of business for want of flour."[26] Even the largest log cabin town in the world couldn't have everything.

All through the lean days of the food shortage, Barnette's association with the Northern Commercial Company was paying off handsomely. In September of 1903 the company put up a fine, new two-story building covered with corrugated iron on Barnette's trading-post ground. That fall, farther downriver on First Avenue, Captain Barnette put up a new home for himself and Mrs. Barnette, away from the store and the rush of business.[27] Along with a new home and a new store, Barnette also had a new position. In November he became the first official mayor of Fairbanks.

The first election to choose a mayor and incorporate the city had been held earlier in the summer when Barnette was on his way back from San Francisco. This election was illegal because approval from Judge Wickersham was needed to run an election for incorporation. The winner of the illegal election was Dr. C.D. "Little Docky" Medill, with 175 votes. One of the members of the six-man council of the provisional government was Frank Cleary, so Captain Barnette's interests were not neglected.[28]

But Barnette wanted to be mayor himself. The town of Fairbanks received a notice from Judge Wickersham providing for an election to be held on November 10, 1903, to decide whether Fairbanks should be incorporated and if so, to choose a city council. An incorporated city could collect money from liquor licenses and levy a poll tax to provide services like fire protection and sewage disposal. An incorporated city would even have the money to start a school for the half-dozen children of school age in the mining camp.

When the votes were counted on November 10, incorporation had passed, as expected. In the voting for the city council members, Barnette had 67 votes, second only to John L. Long who had 73. The custom was that the man with the most votes became mayor, and the next six highest vote getters became city councilmen. Barnette, however, did not want to be second in command in his own town. As the founder of Fairbanks, he thought it was his right to be mayor if he wanted to be. He was prospering in business and could afford to be a public servant. So by pulling a few strings with his cronies who had been elected to the other council seats and collecting on some past favors, Barnette got himself voted in as mayor by the council at its first meeting. As one disgusted election watcher commented, "Mr. Long is certainly the choice of the majority of the voters in Fairbanks, and the people's voice at the polls should have been considered by the council."[29]

Whether the miners liked it or not, Mayor Barnette was sworn in at the first city council meeting on the night of November 11, 1903, and he went to work right away. Barnette brought up the subject of the food shortage and urged that the city government write a letter to the Committee on Territories of the United States Senate asking for relief. The council went along with the idea, and Barnette wrote a long letter the next day to Senator Knute Nelson, chairman of the committee. Describing the bad situation, he pleaded with the senators to "do away with a little red tape" and help them get food from the army post nearby.

"It is useless to theorize as to whom, if anyone, is to blame for the deplorable shortage," the mayor of Fairbanks wrote. If the senators would arrange for the supplies at Fort Gibbon to be sold in Fairbanks, Barnette said he would make sure that the "vultures who speculate in human necessities should have no chance to fatten on the government liberality." Barnette explained that he was not asking for food to be given away but only to be sold at fair market prices. He assured the senators, "No drones of any kind will receive orders for supplies from us."[30] Barnette concluded, "For humanity's sake we beseech you to come to our rescue. Many lives depend upon your favorable and prompt action."[31]

Captain Barnette's passionate letter was somewhat successful in Washington, but not in Fairbanks. A brigadier general in the War Department issued orders to permit the sale of extra provisions at Fort Gibbon and other military posts in Alaska, but the army was not going to ship the food directly to the Tanana. In Fairbanks there was a supposedly "well grounded belief" among certain people that Barnette had set up the food shortage in the first place and somehow was profiting from it. They thought the mayor himself was one of the "vultures who speculate in human necessities." It was rumored that Captain Barnette had "several hundred pounds of flour cached around town, awaiting the time when that article will command the fancy price of $50.00 per sack, to introduce it to the markets." So Barnette's pleading letter to the senators was "looked upon with suspicion, to speak mildly."[32]

Luckily for everyone, there was an "extraordinarily liberal supply of rabbits" and the weather was mild. And as one prospector said, "there were too many men handy with the Winchester to go hungry while there were caribou among the hills."[33] So no one starved that winter. Otherwise Barnette might have been in worse trouble with the miners. But that year there were no threats of violence or attempts to take over his trading post. Perhaps the rumors were caused by nothing more than envy of a successful man.

Captain Barnette was indeed a prominent community leader. At the first big social occasion in Fairbanks, a smoker at the Arctic Brotherhood (the fraternal organization of the north), Barnette was appointed a "marshal." The doors opened at eight o'clock in the evening with a committee standing by to meet the 250 guests and members "with a welcome hand and a cheering bowl."[34] Music came from a phonograph with a large horn, and there was also a six-piece orchestra. "Marshal" Barnette's job at the party was to "preserve order" and to pick out people who had "to pay the penalty for some misdemeanor" by singing a song or telling a story. While half-a-dozen waiters brought around large quantities of fine whiskey and good cigars, a group of six people sang "Farewell My Own True Love," a touching song for those who were so far away from home. Afterwards, J.C. Kellum from Jackson County, Missouri, took the floor. Kellum, a graduate of Harvard (class of 1873), known to everyone as "Judge," entertained the company with a fine rendition of "The Song of the Salmon," a poem about Fairbanks and Chena sung to the tune of the popular song "A Hot Time in the Old Town Tonight." The chorus of the newest local hit went:

> When you hear those corks
> go click, click, click,
> Jump right up and quickly
> take your drink,
> For when the hootch is gone
> you'll never, never think,
> There was a hot time
> in Fairbanks tonight.

The Arctic Brothers at Fairbanks, or ABs, as they called themselves, could not let the occasion go by without poking fun at Chena, where, according to the local humor, the people did nothing all day but catch fish in the Tanana River. Judge Kellum's

"Song of the Salmon" was largely about Chena and the people who lived there, the "Chenese":

> There is a village near our city,
>   and it's nine miles there they say
> Where they catch the wily salmon
>   on a Universal lay,
> And they catch him while he's swimming
>   and they catch him while he drinks,
> That's all there's in this village
>   and it stinks, and stinks, and stinks.
> You can smell them ere
>   you reach the town,
> And the stench will nearly
>   knock you down,
> And the air is thick
>   for miles and miles around,
> But there's a hot time in Fairbanks
>   tonight poor salmon. [35]

As the mayor, postmaster, leading property owner, and biggest business man in Fairbanks, Captain Barnette probably enjoyed "The Song of the Salmon" as much as anyone. The future for Fairbanks was definitely looking brighter all the time. Thirty-two miles of pay streak had been discovered on the creeks. This was encouraging, since only 50 miles had been uncovered in the Klondike after all the time and money spent looking for gold there. [36]

Conditions in the city of Fairbanks were improving as well. Ordinance No. 1 passed by Barnette's city council granted a 10-year telephone franchise to N.A. Fuller of San Francisco, letting him put up as many 35-foot telephone poles as he needed on the south side of the avenues and the west side of the streets. [37] The council also passed ordinances regarding sanitation including the "deposition of garbage and the care of out houses."

For a short time during the winter of 1903-1904, Fairbanks even had a one-teacher, one-room school with 13 pupils — until the money ran out and the school was disbanded. The growth of education would have to wait. [38]

The city moved ahead on fire-protection plans; and in conjunction with a citizen's committee, it hired a night watchman to sound the alarm if he spotted a fire. For the volunteer fire department the city government purchased a 14-inch diameter fire bell and a 15-gallon chemical pump. A street committee of the city council was charged with overseeing the proper marking and surveying of the streets.

Barnette saw no reason why the mayor's family could not share in the benefits of improving his town. He usually found it convenient to have his relatives become his business associates. Over the strenuous objections of some people, a franchise was given to James W. Hill, another brother-in-law of Captain Barnette, granting Hill "electric light privileges" for 25 years and also giving him the right to provide drinking water and steam heat for the city.[39]

In the spring of 1904 Captain Barnette left Fairbanks for about three months on another trip to San Francisco. He wanted to make sure that the Northern Commercial Company's head office arranged to ship in enough food for the summer of 1904. This time there was no doubt in anyone's mind: As soon as the ice went

out, there was going to be a rush to Fairbanks from all over the
Pacific Northwest. In the middle of April the mayor was back
from California with news that his company would ship in from
5,000 to 7,000 tons of supplies as soon as possible.

"My trip has been a most successful one," Barnette explained on
his return. "I went out to impress upon the company the necessity
for getting supplies enough in here, and I have succeeded. Other
wealthy individuals and companies have sought me out and
talked with me about the camp, and have decided to come
here."[40]

Mayor Barnette was delighted to say that his company was
even then building a new boat especially to handle the huge
amount of freight it was going to ship to Fairbanks. Appropri-

ately, the sternwheeler would be called the *Tanana*. It was then under construction in Portland, Oregon, at a cost of $40,000, and would be equipped with all the modern conveniences, such as electric lights and passenger staterooms. The *Tanana* would have accommodations for 50 passengers, a freight capacity of 200 tons, and an engine powerful enough to push a barge carrying another 200 tons.[41]

The Northern Commercial Company was also planning to construct several new buildings in Fairbanks and expand its services to sell full lines of both hardware and machinery. More important, Mayor Barnette said that he too was moving into a new enterprise. He was shipping in a steel vault eight feet high and 10 feet square to be set in five feet of concrete. With the success of his investments in Fairbanks Captain Barnette was well on his way to becoming the wealthiest man in Alaska, and he was going to open his own bank.

7

The American Klondike

Almost overnight, gold turned Barnette's rough frontier outpost into a city of saloons and three-story skyscrapers. From 1903 to 1905 the yearly gold production in Fairbanks increased from $40,000, to $600,000 to $6,000,000.[1] In 1903 Fairbanks was a trading post surrounded by a wooden fence and a field of tree stumps. It was little more than a clearing in the wilderness. Two years later it was home for thousands of people, and was on its way to becoming the largest city in Alaska.[2] A new Dawson City had appeared on the banks of the Chena River, and, in a way no one expected, the old dream of an American Klondike had come true.

A man wrote about Fairbanks in 1904, "To walk down Front Street here one would think that one had been asleep and awaked in Dawson, so far as faces are concerned, for nine-tenths of the people here have been in Dawson."[3] Another visitor who knew the old Klondike crowd had a similar reaction when he visited Fairbanks for the first time a year later in 1905.

"My first impression was that I had alighted by some way in Dawson, for in looking around me I saw the same signs hanging from the buildings, the same old horses and dogs on the streets, and the same old boys and girls in the saloons, doing the same old things for a living that they have been doing ever since they first struck the trail in '97."[4] He noted that many of the old millionaires from the Klondike had come on hard times and that even the new Dawson City could not turn back the clock. "Some of the mighty kings of Bonanza Creek are playing a lone hand here. It is surprising how the mighty have fallen in the last two or three years."[5]

When the boats of 1904 came to Fairbanks, they brought half of Dawson City with them, including the miners and their mining equipment, and businessmen with their entire businesses. But Mayor Barnette's town still had to face the greatest threat to its existence, the reborn town of Chena. If Barnette had originally gotten off the *Lavelle Young* at the mouth of the Chena, as he had wished, Fairbanks would probably have been located at the site of Chena on the Tanana River. But a natural advantage or a good location is far from being the most important factor in the affairs of men.

Earlier in the winter of 1904 Chena appeared to be dying, and to the people in the world's largest log cabin town, the name of Chena was a joke. According to one census only 23 people were living in Chena at the end of 1903.[6] However, three men from Dawson City, Martin Harrais, Frank Smith, and John Joslin, had plans to change all that. In the late fall of 1903 they quietly examined the Tanana mines and made plans to build a railroad to the gold mines from wherever the steamboats would land the freight. The deep drift mines would be profitable only if machinery could be hauled in to speed up the work; and with the tremendous prices being charged by the teamsters and freighters, a railroad seemed a natural investment. Harrais, Smith, and Joslin thought that Chena would be the only logical terminus for the railroad.

The gold production of a mining claim was directly dependent on the cost of getting supplies and equipment to the creek. Cheaper freight rates meant that more and bigger machinery could be used to bring the claim a higher rate of return. The cost of moving a large piece of equipment from Fairbanks to the creeks was prohibitive. A five-horsepower boiler made in Pennsylvania cost $500 in Fairbanks. But at the going summer freighting rate, it cost another $325 just to move that little boiler to a claim 25 miles from town. If the freighters could have moved a big $3,000, 50-horsepower boiler weighing six tons, the charge to haul it to the creeks could easily have been another $3,000.[7]

In the summertime the trails to the creeks could become almost impassable. A heavy wagon pulled by six horses and carrying a ton of freight could come close to drowning in a sea of mud and mosquitoes. Horses would sometimes sink so far into the mud that they had to be pulled out with long ropes and teams of horses in tandem; and some actually sank so deep that they suffocated in the muck. A man on Cleary Creek once told a story to illustrate how bad the trails were outside Fairbanks. He said he was walking along when he saw a pack strapped to a mule which was almost sunk out of sight in the mud, but he paid no attention because it was a "common enough sight." A short distance away, however, he saw a hat lying on the ground and picked it up.

"Confound you, let my hat alone," said a voice from below. The storyteller then noticed a man's head.

"What are you doing there?" he asked the man in the mud.

"Speak low, don't give me away," whispered the man. "I'm stealing a ride on Hadley's stage."[8]

Martin Harrais, John Joslin, and Frank Smith may not have picked up any hats off the ground, but the richness of the mines and the poor freighting conditions convinced them of the practicality of a railroad. The three had been sent to the Tanana by John Joslin's younger brother, Falcon Joslin, a Dawson City lawyer and promoter. Falcon Joslin had just completed his first narrow-gauge railroad, the 12-mile Coal Creek Coal Mine Railroad below Dawson City.

The Joslin survey party in the Tanana decided that the cheapest and most profitable route for the Tanana Mines Railway would be to run the line from the town of Chena, the head of navigation on the Tanana River, 21 miles to Gilmore, below Pedro Dome. They thought that Fairbanks was nothing but a "townsite boom" and that the railroad should bypass it entirely. In their opinion Chena "could not help but be the town" because it was on a better site and could be reached easily by boats of any size throughout the summer.[9]

Only when the steamboats started bringing loads of people and supplies up the Tanana River in the early summer of 1904 did Barnette realize how serious a threat Chena was going to be. The Chena River was so shallow in May of that year that no boat drawing more than two feet of water could get within four miles of Fairbanks. The big sternwheelers had no choice but to unload at Chena. If Chena was the head of navigation for most of the year, why not locate the main settlement there, even though it was farther from the heart of the creeks? The Tanana Mines Railroad would offset the disadvantage of being too far from the mines, and then Chena would have it all over Fairbanks.

John Joslin and Martin Harrais decided to beat Captain Barnette at his own game of town building. On brown wrapping paper they had platted the survey line of the Tanana Mines Railway, running directly to the foot of Pedro Dome. The proposed line did not pass within five miles of Fairbanks.[10] Joslin became the trustee of the Chena townsite, and Martin Harrais became the first mayor of Chena. In the years to come it was estimated that Harrais alone would spend roughly $86,000 promoting the development of the town.[11]

The shallow river and the threat of the railroad put Mayor Barnette and even Judge Wickersham into a panic.

"A very blue day, yesterday and today, for many," Wickersham wrote in his diary on May 31, 1904, "as the river is so low that the boats cannot get up to Fairbanks and our Chena friends are knocking this town effectively on account of it."[12] A "mosquito fleet" of small boats was moving freight up the river to Fairbanks for two cents a pound. Even Captain Barnette himself was working day and night hauling freight on the *Isabelle* over the seven-mile stretch of river between Chena and Fairbanks. The mayor of Fairbanks was convinced that if he could keep the supplies coming to Fairbanks for another week, the water would rise and the crisis would be over.

For the town of Chena, too, it was a crucial situation. Belt and Hendricks had leased out their own shallow-draft boat, the *Tanana Chief*, to A.W. Williams, who started using it to haul freight up the Chena River to Fairbanks. They ordered him to stop. When Williams refused, they brought suit against him and forcibly tied the *Tanana Chief* up at Chena. Williams brought a counter-suit, asking $500 a day damages.[13] Someone suggested that the people of Chena should go into the kidnapping business as a new way to promote the growth of their town. As it was, Chena and Fairbanks had almost declared war on each other, but the battle was a short one.

The last week of May and the first week of June in 1904 assured the future of Fairbanks. Despite the hazard of the shallow river, the wave of new settlers getting off the boats kept coming to Mayor Barnette's town. His city was going to survive.

If the Chena River was too shallow, the Fairbanks City Council would simply make it deeper. To raise the water level, the city of Fairbanks subscribed about $12,000 to divert the Tanana River directly into the Chena.[14] Representatives of all the biggest businesses in Fairbanks and Judge Wickersham himself were on the committee to oversee the enterprise, which they hoped would make the river deep enough so that boats could always reach Fairbanks. More than just improving the river, which was not too successful, the city of Fairbanks would bypass the Chena River entirely with the help of an unlikely ally, the Tanana Mines Railroad.

Falcon Joslin arrived at Chena in the fall of 1904, hoping to build at least 10 miles of his railroad before freeze-up. Provisions for the workers, hay and grain for the horses, tents, wagons, scrapers, wheelbarrows, and tools were all en route by riverboat. Also on the boats and river barges were 550 tons of 35-pound steel rails.[15] No definite public announcement had yet been made about the route the railroad would take, but by late August, John Joslin had been saying that maybe the rails would not run directly from Chena to the mines as he had originally planned. The shallowness of the river had been less of an obstacle than he had previously thought, and Fairbanks had grown at a tremendous rate during the summer. The railroad company wished "to do the transportation business of the district in such a manner as to leave no encouraging opening for an opposition line to step in and compete."[16]

Falcon Joslin examined the town sites, and as the president of the Tanana Mines Railway Company, he decided that the railroad should serve both Chena and Fairbanks, with the company's headquarters located at Chena.[17] Joslin explained that he did not want "to cast favors or prejudice with one town or the other" and that he would lay eight miles of track connecting Chena and Fairbanks. The point at which the line running north from Chena met the line running west from Fairbanks was known as the Junction. From the Junction, the main line of the Tanana Mines Railroad would continue on out to the creeks. The first section of the railroad which Joslin wished to complete was the Valley Division of the Tanana Mines Railway, running eight miles from Chena to Fairbanks.

The railroad was not seen by Captain Barnette or Judge Wickersham as an absolute blessing. In their eyes the project was still an enterprise of the town of Chena, and they suspected that with the railroad's offices and construction headquarters located at Chena, that town would benefit most from its construction. In the long run, however, Fairbanks prospered even more because of the railroad, since the rails made the question of the navigability of the Chena River academic. A large part of the freight carried by

By 1905 the city has a new power plant, a fine three-story building, a $10,000 bridge, and a row of saloons and restaurants along the river.

(University of Alaska Archives, Charles Bunnell Collection)

the railroad after its completion was known as "steamboat freight," or freight that would normally have gone up the Chena by boat had the river been deep enough. Instead of Chena becoming more important in its own right, the town became a transfer point for freight and passengers about to take the 45-minute train ride to Fairbanks.[18]

In its heyday in 1904-1905, the city of Chena was almost as large as Fairbanks. On the main streets of Chena, which were named after states in the union such as Iowa, Maine and Washington, stood a solid half-mile of good frame buildings. Like Fairbanks, Chena had its own electric light plant, a telephone system, a jail, a hospital, a schoolhouse, a 500-seat public amusement hall, large docks along the waterfront, a big railroad yard, several newspapers, a police department, and a fire department. Yet

while Fairbanks kept growing, Chena began to disappear. By 1907 Fairbanks had a population of 5,000 people, while only 450 people were left at the "head of navigation."

Less than 10 years later Chena was almost totally abandoned. The first mayor of Chena, Martin Harrais, who helped lay out the railroad in 1903, was one of the contractors who in 1916 dismantled many of the empty buildings at Chena for shipment to Nenana and Fairbanks. A newspaperman reported, "Martin Harrais, the father of Chena, who furnished the material or the money to build most all of Chena, is now engaged in superintending the destruction of the buildings he was instrumental in some way in constructing. Every time he tears off a board of Chena he feels as if he was committing an indignity upon an old friend, but times change and population moves on, and there is money in supplying a demand, so Martin keeps right on with the work and lets Chena go at that."[19] In 1920 the railroad tracks to Chena were torn up, and the town was dead once and for all.

Long before that, however, the city of Fairbanks, and

Barnette's personal business affairs were booming; and while Chena began to go downhill, Barnette's star continued to rise. In 1904 he sold his remaining one-third interest in his trading post to the Northern Commercial Company, deeding to NC almost all the land covered by his trading post site. He kept two lots in his wife's name, one of which was next to the courthouse and was the site of Captain Barnette's new bank: the Fairbanks Banking and Safe Deposit Vault Company.

Barnette opened his bank on September 9, 1904, with $25,000 capital from the sale of his post to the Northern Commercial Company. R.C. Wood, Barnette's cashier, was responsible for the day to day operations of the bank. Before Barnette opened his bank all banking had been done at the Northern Commercial Company. Now the big eight-by-ten-foot vault Barnette had shipped in to Fairbanks was set in concrete to give "protection to the citizens and miners — a place to deposit valuables in safety against fire and other casualties."[20] As the residents of Fairbanks learned much later, Barnette's bank was itself a dangerous place to put their money.

Captain Barnette made money with his money, both in his bank and with his mining property. He put up the $25,000 capital to start the bank and served as its president. For providing the capital, he would get two-thirds of the profits. Since Barnette knew nothing about banking, his cashier, who handled all the business, would receive one-third of the profits. As the gold from the mines poured into town, the bank became an extremely profitable business. Within a few years Captain Barnette's $25,000 had grown to $200,000. As the bank grew Barnette had his brother-in-law, James Hill, come in as another cashier. Hill, who had earlier received the city franchise for electric power and steam heat, was a former cashier and auditor for the Northern Commercial Company. He joined Barnette's bank as vice-president, and the arrangement was changed so that Barnette got 50 percent of the bank's profits, while Hill and Wood received 25 percent apiece.[21]

E.T. Barnette made as much money on his mining property as he did with his bank. One observer of banker Barnette who did not care for the way he obtained his mining claims once declared, "it was always beneath Cap's dignity to stake anything less than a whole creek."[22] Barnette had located claims "broadcast" by using the power of attorney for his relatives in Ohio, by having his employees stake them for him, and by trading and purchasing claims outright. Barnette's many claims were the subject of never-ending legal battles, and soon he was "either plaintiff or defendant in more law suits than he could keep books on."[23] Such was the way of a successful businessman.

As a man who did his mining with his pencil, Captain Barnette was unpopular with those who mined with a shovel. Technical questions about what actually constituted a "discovery" of gold and about Barnette's use of the power of attorney were favorite subjects for debate in the courtroom and in the newspapers. To counter some of the adverse publicity, Barnette bought out the *Fairbanks Daily News*, which lost a lot of money under his control, but regularly printed highly laudatory articles about its owner. After one such article, C.C. Pyne, who had been around the Tanana Valley as long as Felix Pedro and had been the first man to tell Barnette of Pedro's gold strike in 1902, felt he had to respond with a letter to the editor of the opposition newspaper.

Pyne wrote that "anybody who knows the Captain will not dispute" the fact that he is "a thorough frontiersman" and very successful. "But as to this camp, with the Captain it was fate, followed by unusual luck; he was all in, and had to stay here. I was here when the Captain landed here in August, '01, and I have been here ever since.

"Now, I am willing to allow any man his just dues," Pyne continued, "but you will have to show me where Barnette ever sank a hole, or caused one to be sunk, prior to 1904. After that I believe he was guilty of having some holes put to bedrock, but that was after the question of discovery became important, and prior to that I know of no man in the camp who staked on the wholesale plan as did Captain Barnette, and held his claims by virtue of his stakes alone."[24]

The disapproval of an old-timer like Pyne did not carry weight in court. Barnette's lawyer was the man considered by many to be the sharpest attorney in Alaska, John L. McGinn. He was the brother of a famous lawyer, Henry McGinn of Portland, who, it was learned later, had known E.T. Barnette years earlier in Oregon under circumstances that were not so friendly. When Barnette and John McGinn brought a claim into court, it was always staked "with a fence around it," — sewn up tight legally. "The result was that when Barnette's titles were attacked in court by those who coveted," an admiring account of Barnette stated, "he usually won the decision."[25]

The captain had another powerful friend in the courtroom, Judge Wickersham, who heard three cases brought by Barnette in

1904. The captain was the winner of one case in which Wickersham denied the loser's request for a new trial. In a different suit Judge Wickersham overturned the verdict of a jury which ruled against Barnette: the judge ordered a new trial on the grounds that "the evidence does not support the verdict as rendered by the jury."[26]

Allegations that Wickersham was too friendly with Captain Barnette both in and out of the courtroom plagued the judge during his years on the bench and later when he became Alaska's Delegate in Congress. But the relationship between the two men was always a little uneasy, since neither was content to play second fiddle to the other. Undoubtedly they helped each other a great deal, but they were never close personal friends.

On one occasion when a mining claim of Barnette's was involved in some litigation and the case was to be decided in Wickersham's court, the judge wrote in his diary that Barnette had hinted he would make him part owner of a valuable claim after his term as judge was over. The offer was an outright bribe, and the judge said he indignantly walked away. "Next time I'll roast him," Wickersham wrote in his diary. "Some men are so miserly that it amounts to dishonesty."[27]

Captain Barnette had no cause at all to be miserly with those who could help him, because everything he touched seemed to turn to gold. The idle mining claims he had staked in the early years he could lease out with no risk on his part and get a good return. For instance, when he leased the lower half of Discovery Claim on Chatham Creek, the lease agreement stated that Barnette was to receive 30 percent of the gold produced, a standard rate for a leased mining claim. The big advantage was that Barnette could have all the work done by someone else — cabins built and shafts dug — and still be paid from the proceeds. The improvements on the claim remained as the "absolute property" of the man who leased the claim, and any time the workers struck an especially rich pay streak which Barnette would like to work with his own employees, the captain could cancel the lease agreement.[28]

With his extensive holdings of mining ground and ownership of the first bank in Fairbanks, Barnette made money on both ends, and as the total gold production of the district increased, he became an extremely wealthy man. The banking business was so good that two other banks opened early in 1905: The First National Bank, established by Sam Bonnifield, a successful

Floodwaters from the Chena River and runaway logs from the sawmill upstream threaten the businesses on First Avenue during the disastrous flood of 1905, caused by Fairbanks's new Cushman Street bridge. To avert the danger to downtown Fairbanks, workers had to dynamite the impressive structure. The Turner Street bridge replaced the Cushman Street bridge after the flood.

Juneau mine operator turned gambler in Dawson City; and the Washington-Alaska Bank, with John Scram as president and Falcon Joslin of the Tanana Mines Railway as vice-president.[29]

In the spring of 1905, Barnette was re-elected mayor, but it was rumored that he had his sights on a loftier position and was lobbying to be appointed governor of Alaska. Barnette was, after all, the mayor of the largest and fastest-growing city in Alaska and was the owner of a bank, a newspaper, and numerous gold mines. Though he was said to have made a trip back to Washington, D.C., to promote his candidacy, he never became Governor Barnette. He was far too stubborn to be very popular with the voters, and his future was not in politics. In 1904 the captain and Mrs. Barnette had had a baby girl, their first child and the fourth white child born in Fairbanks. With a sense of history, they called their daughter Virginia Barnette, for Virginia Dare, the first English child born to the settlers of Virginia in the New World three centuries earlier.[30]

A founding father could also enjoy the finer things in life. Barnette had always been interested in fast horses, and now as a prosperous banker he could afford to have his own. For $60,000 he purchased a large stock farm in the blue-grass country of Kentucky. At one time he was said to be the owner of the fastest two-year-old trotter in the United States, a horse named Virginia Barnette.

One year, on an extended visit to the East Coast, Mrs. Barnette and her sister accompanied the captain to Washington, D.C., and New York. They also took a pleasant automobile trip from Buffalo through Pennsylvania, to the stock farm in Lexington, Kentucky. After six weeks on the horse farm, Captain Barnette and a group of other wealthy businessmen went on a trip to Mexico to examine some huge tracts of land in the public domain that the Mexican government was interested in selling.

Before its revolution early in this century, Mexico was a haven for American businessmen, and U.S. investments south of the border amounted to more than $1 billion. Huge American coffee and sugar plantations were common, and it was said that the Hearst newspaper family owned a tract of land "about the size of Maryland and Delaware combined."[31]

American investors were treated like royalty in Mexico. When Barnette and the other businessmen sailed down the west coast of Mexico to what the captain described as "one of the prettiest harbors in the world," Acapulco, they were met by the governor of

A three-story building at the corner of First and Cushman explodes in flames on May 22, 1906, just a year after the destructive flood.
(University of Alaska Archives, Charles Bunnell Collection)

the state of Guerro, who gave them a military escort. After looking over the lands for sale, they went on to Mexico City by boat and train, to enjoy a holiday and fiesta, and Barnette witnessed a bullfight.[32]

Sometime after this trip Barnette began buying Mexican property. He eventually purchased a plantation totaling more than 18,700 acres for $75,000, about four dollars an acre. His partner in the Mexican land deal was a man named Ward, who was to manage and develop the plantation. Barnette owned 51 percent of the plantation, while Ward owned the minority interest. The project was financed entirely by Captain Barnette, and sometimes he was putting as much as $10,000 a month into the plantation to clear the land and plant bananas, coconuts, and other tropical crops.

With the money he had made in Fairbanks, Captain Barnette built his own private city in Mexico.[33] The estate was a large-scale operation. Barnette had a large stone house, and his business

Within minutes the entire city is ablaze.
(University of Alaska Archives, Charles Bunnell Collection)

headquarters were located in a magnificent brick building with a patio, cistern well, large open markets and squares, a library, and its own refrigeration and electric light plant. He also constructed a cold-storage warehouse; in addition, the estate had a blacksmith shop, a harness shop, a wood-working plant, "other necessary plants for handling, sharpening, and making tools," a large store with $10,000 worth of supplies, and grain warehouses.

The Barnette plantation had 1,300 head of stock, including horses, cattle, oxen, and mules, and within a few years almost 6,000 acres of land were under cultivation.[34] Barnette had more than 600 Mexican employees on his plantation. He could afford to have 600 men on the estate because they were only paid 31¼ cents a day, which was good money for Mexico.

Barnette's hacienda was small compared to most, but like all of them, it was a feudal society. With the big cigars that he loved to smoke and his Panama hat, Captain Barnette was as powerful on

94

his estate as any plantation owner in Mexico. But for the present his first concern was still his investments in the town he had founded in Alaska. Fairbanks, by making him a millionaire several times over, had made possible all the horses, the ranches, the farm in Kentucky, and the plantation in Mexico.

Fairbanks had become a most imposing little city, as approached from the river. Beyond the First Avenue saloons and stores with names like the Monte Carlo, the Senate, and the Tanana, hundreds of log cabins were spread out in a fan a dozen blocks deep away from the river. Prostitution was tolerated only on Fourth Avenue, known as "the Row." To protect the sensibilities of the more respectable women and children, a high board fence with a gate in it was put up on each end of the block between Cushman and Barnette Streets — but not before the city council had a long debate over where the fence should have a gate, so as not to hurt business downtown.[35]

The most impressive structure in Fairbanks in 1905 was the newly completed $10,000 bridge across the Chena River. A good bridge was essential to the city and had been vigorously supported by Captain Barnette. Downtown Fairbanks was cut off from the trails to the gold mines by the Chena River, and the bridge was the city's lifeline. Less than two weeks after the great bridge was completed, however, the Cushman Street bridge almost destroyed Fairbanks.

A big pile of driftwood had jammed on the upriver side of the Wendell Street bridge, the smaller $5,000 bridge that had recently been constructed upstream from Cushman Street. Suddenly, at 4:30 P.M. on June 30, 1905, the Wendell Street bridge gave way. Shouts rang down the river, "Look out, the Wendell Street bridge has collapsed!" A reporter on the riverbank wrote, "The scene that followed will be forever remembered in Fairbanks."[36]

The platform of the Wendell Street bridge fell into the water and stayed upright as the bridge collapsed. Breaking into three pieces, the remains of the bridge came roaring down the Chena ripping loose acres of log booms from a sawmill and heading straight for the Cushman Street bridge. When the main section of the runaway bridge smashed into the Cushman Street bridge, water shot up 20 feet in the air, and thousands of logs piled into the bridge. The logs "twisted and wrenched and fairly screamed under the fearful pressure of water."

The Cushman Street bridge held, and there was a universal sigh of relief. "She will stand," they said.[37] But the Cushman Street bridge, the wreckage of the old Wendell Street bridge, and the thousands of logs in the water dammed up the Chena River and flooded the city. Most serious of all was the fact that the river started to cut around the dam by eating away a new channel right down First Avenue. Foot by foot, the main street of Fairbanks started to disappear and buildings closest to the river were abandoned out of fear that they would be washed away. The day after the Wendell Street bridge washed out, the situation was dismal.

"Saturday morning the Cushman Street bridge was standing in the center of a raging torrent, a grim witness of the engineer's ability and at the same time the cause of all the damage that had been wrought."[38] The river was pouring through a cut 40 feet wide and 400 feet long where First Avenue had once been.

To stop the river from cutting through the heart of downtown Fairbanks, workers had to dynamite the Cushman Street bridge, and they finally succeeded in blowing it out of the water.

The scare was over, and laborers began to dump driftwood and dirt into the cut, but it was months before most of the gash was filled in. Total damage to the city was $50,000, but if the work-

Fairbanks News

VOLUME 2   FAIRBANKS, ALASKA, MAY 23, 1906.   NUMBER 20

Fire Can Not Stop Fairbanks

New and Better Town Arising From Smoking Ruins

While the old ruins of the business section of Fairbanks are still smoking, a new and better Fairbanks is springing into being. At an early hour this morning the burnt zone, representing the heart of the business section and totaling fully a million dollars, was peopled with busy workers.

Before noon today several places had opened for business in temporary quarters. Without a single exception all of the property owners will rebuild. Ruins and debris are being cleared away on every side today to make place for the foundations of new buildings.

"Certainly we shall rebuild," was the matter-of-fact answer given a News reporter in all cases.

they had put up all of their money into building and furnished it as one of the finest hotels in the north, and were getting in shape where they could begin to make money. Then, too, their building was more or less isolated, and could have been saved with plenty of water, but the furnace across the street proved to be too hot.

BUTTE CAFE TO OPEN.

Tommy Gamble and H. T. Bentley, of the Butte cafe, started men at work this morning, and will shortly be open for business. They had improved their former place from time to time, so that it covered a full lot and was one of the best stocked restaurants in the city. Their loss will reach fully 8,000 thousand. They will rebuild on as large a scale as

will rebuild at once. His loss amounts to nearly 10,000 thousand.

FIRST MEN ON GROUND.

Bert Epler, of the Senate saloon, was one of the first to have men on the ground. His loss is estimated at 12,000 thousand.

Bob Geis and George Herington, who owned the fine Fairbanks block, where the fire started, will put up a temporary structure for their saloon on the corner. They will decide later about building another block.

The block was occupied downstairs by themselves, by Isaacs Bros. the clothers who saved most of their goods, and have opened temporarily in their ware-house; by Anderson Bros., the well known

"Without a single exception all of the property owners will rebuild," reports the Fairbanks News the morning following the 1906 fire which destroyed downtown Fairbanks. (University of Alaska Archives)

men had not succeeded in removing the dam when they did, the river could have torn apart the entire city center.

Less than a year later, downtown Fairbanks was completely destroyed, not by flood, but by fire. On May 22, 1906, a fire that started in a dentist's office in the largest building in town, at the corner of First and Cushman, turned the structure into a torch three stories tall. Within 42 minutes the city center from Turner Street to Lacey, and from First to Third avenues, was gone. The city was made of dry wooden buildings, with sawdust insulation if any, and the fire was impossible to control. Fortunately, a wind blew the flames towards the river; otherwise the damage would have been even more widespread. Captain Barnette was luckier than most. The other two banks in town burned down, but his Fairbanks Banking Company was saved. The bank's employees hung heavy, wet, woolen blankets over the eaves of the building and kept dousing it with water until the flames died down.[39]

This time the damages were estimated to be over $1.5 million. Some suggested that since the major portion of downtown Fairbanks was destroyed, the town should now move to Chena, but that possibility had long since disappeared. Visitors from California said the damage to Fairbanks was not nearly as serious as that suffered by San Francisco, which had been leveled by the famous earthquake and fire of 1906 a month earlier. Like San Francisco, Fairbanks would rebuild. Before the embers had died out in Fairbanks, dozens of businessmen were making plans for their new buildings and ordering the lumber they would need.

Barnette's city was not going to fold up and disappear like countless other gold rush towns across the West.

One year after the devastating fire of 1906, the new "Tanana Directory" of Fairbanks and the other towns in the Tanana Valley stated, "A stranger approaching Fairbanks on a steamer at night, and first sighting the city in the distance, would be greeted with a sight he would never forget."[40] Lit up with electric lights, the city glared like a "good sized metropolis," where half-a-dozen years earlier there had been an uninhabited valley. For Captain Barnette business could not have been going better.

Then came November 27, 1906, when the mayor of Fairbanks, millionaire banker, land baron, and would-be governor of Alaska sat on the witness stand in a courtroom in Seattle. After first denying it, Captain Barnette broke down and admitted under cross-examination that he was an ex-convict from the state of Oregon.

8

Ex-Convict

The golden spike of the Tanana Mines Railway was driven on July 17, 1905. A picture of the event shows a crowd of people standing on the railroad track surrounding Mrs. Isabelle Barnette, who is wearing a large, fancy hat and a long, dark dress. She is holding the golden spike up in the air with her right hand and smiling broadly. Engraved on the 40-ounce spike made of gold mined in the Tanana diggings were the date and the inscription, "Driven by Mrs. E.T. Barnette." After the ceremony Falcon Joslin, president of the Tanana Mines Railway, gave the golden spike to Mrs. Barnette as a souvenir.[1]

Joslin was standing to Mrs. Barnette's right. On her left was Judge Wickersham, holding a copy of the speech he had given to celebrate the occasion. In his address Wickersham explained his racial theory of progress and railway building. The judge claimed that even with the millions of dollars the United States government was giving to the Philippines to help the Filipinos build railroads, the Anglo-Saxons of Alaska would build more miles of railways than in all of that huge Asian country.[2]

With his hands folded contentedly in front of him, Captain Barnette appears to be standing to the left of the racial railway philosopher. Barnette seems to be nearly a head taller than Wickersham, but as usual we can see less of the captain than of

Smiling broadly, Mrs. Isabelle Barnette holds the 40-ounce golden spike for the Tanana Valley Railroad in 1905. Judge Wickersham, who spoke at the ceremony, stands to her left, with a man who looks like Captain Barnette (his face obscured by a lady's hat) on the left side of the judge.

anyone else. Barnette's face is partly obscured by the large hat worn by the lady standing in front of him.

Falcon Joslin had hoped to have the golden spike ceremony on the Fourth of July, but the celebration was postponed for two weeks because of the damage caused by the 1905 flood. With the small, wood-burning locomotive and the coach that had arrived by riverboat a few days earlier, the railroad gave free train rides to thousands of people. Some of the older miners hadn't seen a train in years. A few of the frightened sourdoughs had to be blindfolded and backed into the box cars to take their free ride, but they later bought tickets and rode back and forth on every train between Fairbanks and Chena.[3]

Even though the engine was the size of a toy compared to the huge locomotives on the trans-continental lines, the Tanana Mines Railway was a symbol of American civilization, the "up-to-date railway Anglo-Saxon civilization," as Wickersham called it. In less than four years the wilderness where Barnette had been stranded all alone had been tamed by a railroad.

Several weeks later Captain and Mrs. Barnette, with their one-year-old daughter Virginia and a nurse, were ready to leave for a visit to the United States. They planned to stop at the big fair being held that summer in Portland, Oregon, before going on to Barnette's old home in Akron, Ohio. The *Fairbanks News* announced the rest of Barnette's plans: "After that they will visit the national capital, where Captain Barnette will remain until the opening session of Congress, looking after the needs of the Tanana. He will go armed with credentials from the leading organizations of this place, and these, together with his personal knowledge of the conditions as they exist here, and the further fact that he is one of the pioneers of the camp and among its most prominent men of today, will make him a valuable friend in placing before the legislators the needs of Interior Alaska."[4]

The Barnette family left Fairbanks on the steamer *Rock Island* at 8 P.M., on August 7, 1905. Many friends were on hand to wish them bon voyage. It is not known whether the Barnettes actually did go to see the fair in Portland on their way to Ohio and Washington, D.C., in 1905. If they did visit Portland, the trip could have been a frightening one for Captain Barnette because in 1888, by a decree of the governor of the state, E.T. Barnette had been banished forever from the state of Oregon.

In Fairbanks the story of Barnette's arrest and conviction for larceny in 1886, when he was sentenced to four years in the Oregon Penitentiary, came out during the course of a suit brought by James H. Causten against Barnette in 1906. Causten had been the man who made possible Barnette's trip up the Tanana on the *Lavelle Young* in 1901 after Barnette's boat, the *Arctic Boy*, was wrecked at St. Michael. After the wreck Barnette did not have enough money to pay the $6,000 freight bill necessary to hire the *Lavelle Young*. Causten had endorsed three notes to enable Barnette and his partner, Charles Smith, to cover their freighting costs, and in return Causten was to receive "one-third of all mining and other property acquired" and one-third of the proceeds from the sale of Barnette's $20,000 worth of trading goods.[5]

In 1906, about a year after the driving of the Tanana Mines Railway golden spike, Causten brought suit in King County Superior Court in Seattle. Causten demanded that "he was an equal partner and entitled to one-half of all the property, real and personal, that Barnette had acquired" from the time that he arrived at the new town site in 1901.[6]

The court contest that followed was a long and bitter one.

Barnette claimed that he had not violated his 1901 contract with Causten. He said that Causten was entitled to receive only a one-third interest of the mining property that Barnette obtained during the winter of 1901-1902 and one-third of the net profits from the sale of his trade goods. The captain said he had not obtained any property during that time. He also claimed that he had not made any profits from the sale of his trade goods because of heavy costs and the fact that Frank Cleary had supposedly embezzled $14,000 — although he had refused to bring legal action against his brother-in-law. In addition, Barnette contended that his contract with Causten had expired in May of 1902, when Causten "refused to proceed further with the venture, stating that he did not desire to give up his position with the government, which was a certainty, for something uncertain. . . ."[7]

A supporter of Barnette's wrote, "Nothing was heard of Causten until after Captain Barnette had acquired a vast fortune. This fortune was acquired by Captain Barnette as the result of his own efforts, ability and capital."[8] Causten admitted that years had gone by during which he had made no attempt to continue supporting Barnette's venture. But the former customs collector maintained that the 1901 contract was still in force, and that contract made him a full partner. Though he never had to give a penny to Barnette — the captain paid for the notes Causten signed for on schedule — Causten claimed he was entitled to fully half of what Barnette had earned in the last five years.

The case of Causten vs. Barnette dragged on for two and a half years in a Seattle courtroom before it was settled, but one of the most important days of the trial was November 27, 1906, when Captain Barnette was testifying on the witness stand. In an effort to show what kind of a man Barnette really was and give support to their charge that he had cheated their client, Causten's attorneys had done some checking into Barnette's past. They asked the captain if he had ever been in Oregon. "Barnette denied he had ever been in that state," an account of the trial read the next day. "Finally when the records of the Oregon Penitentiary were produced, Barnette admitted that in 1886 he had been convicted of larceny by bailee. Barnette then told the entire story omitting nothing and seemed to be relieved when he had concluded his statement."[9]

In June of 1886 23-year-old E.T. Barnette was in the Spelamachine mines country of British Columbia with a plan to "mark out and take up a town site" if the mines were rich enough.

Barnette met a man named George De Wolf; and on Barnette's suggestion, they became partners in a ranching and horse-trading venture. The two were experienced horsemen, and together they drove 100 head of horses across the Rockies through Crows Nest Pass to Calgary. They spent the summer of 1886 moving the horses from town to town and selling them. In the fall, with all their original stock gone, Barnette and De Wolf rode south toward the American border. They headed toward Idaho Territory and northern Washington Territory to open a stock ranch. About 12 miles north of the international boundary, however, Barnette told De Wolf that someone had stolen out of his saddle bag the $2,300 they had made from selling the horses. Barnette showed his partner that a rolled-up piece of an Indian blanket had been put in the place where the money had been.

Two trains "breathing smoke and fire" meet at the junction of the Tanana Mines Railway, where the line from Chena joins the mainline to Fairbanks. The railroad, by hauling needed mining equipment to the gold fields, speeded up extraction of the gold, and the growth of Fairbanks. (Author's Collection)

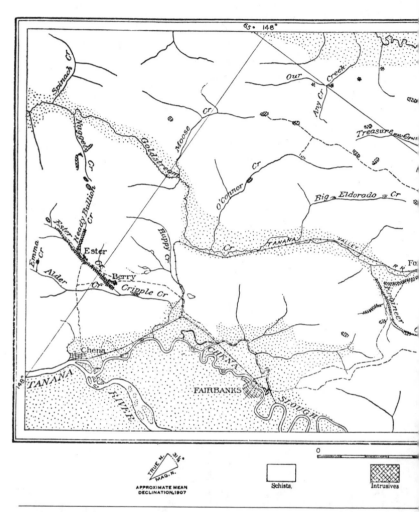

They concluded that an Indian must have stolen the money, and the two of them decided that there was no use going back to look for it. De Wolf went to Dayton in Washington Territory to promote their ranching scheme, and Barnette headed south towards Pendleton, Oregon, where he was to wire his brother in Akron, Ohio, to ask him to send the $2,800 he owed him.

When Barnette and De Wolf met again in Dayton, De Wolf accused his partner of stealing the $2,300. Barnette now had a big bankroll. He admitted that the money had not come from his brother in Akron, but he claimed that all summer long he had had $2,000 of his own money stitched in his shirt. Somehow De Wolf

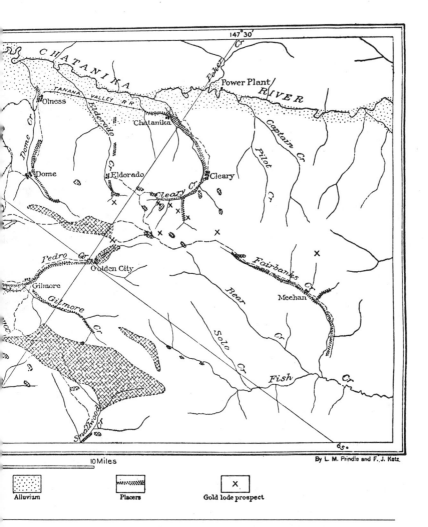

Alluvium

Placers

X
Gold lode prospect

10 Miles

By L. M. Prindle and F. J. Katz

A map of the Fairbanks mining district published in 1911 shows the route of the Tanana Valley Railroad, which connected the town with the surrounding gold camps. (U.S. Geological Survey)

learned that Barnette had sent a letter from Pendleton to a bank in Portland, asking it to change $2,000 in Canadian money for American currency. A check with the bank confirmed that the $2,000 in Canadian money consisted of the identical bills that were missing from the saddlebag and that the United States currency Barnette had received in return was the money he was now claiming he had carried stitched in his shirt all summer.[10]

A wagon train waits at Fox Station on the Tanana Valley Railroad.

De Wolf had Barnette arrested in Washington Territory, and the sheriff took him to Portland to be tried. The *Morning Oregonian* of Portland was indignant. In an article headlined "A Swindler," the newspaper described Mr. George De Wolf of Liverpool as a mining expert who had been swindled by Barnette. All the newspaper knew was that Barnette was a "real estate man from Akron, Ohio," and that he formerly lived in Dayton, Washington Territory. The article asked, "Does any man around these parts know the record of Barnett (sic)?"[11]

Throughout his life E.T. Barnette was always a mystery man, moving in the shadows. But for a person who seemed to come out of nowhere, Barnette had too many enemies. During the course of his trial in Portland the newspaper reported, "A gentleman arrived here from Spokane yesterday, too late to testify in the case, who says Barnett (sic) swindled him out of a lot of horses and barrels of whiskey."[12]

When the jury's verdict came in on Barnette's trial, the *Morning Oregonian* gleefully announced, "A Swindler Convicted." The newspaper described the scene in the courtroom. "Friday night, when the case was given to the jury, Barnett (sic) assumed an air of bravado, turned good naturedly to his counsel and smiled.

Yesterday when the jury came in, and on their verdict being read, Barnett (sic) turned rather uneasily in his chair, and the smile of the evening before was not forthcoming. He immediately recovered himself, and glancing toward the baliff (sic), signified his intention of returning to his quarters in the county jail."[13]

Barnette was sentenced to four years in the Oregon Penitentiary. His lawyers fought his conviction all the way to the Oregon Supreme Court, which upheld the original verdict. After a "very exhaustive and able argument for a rehearing" by Barnette's lawyers, the Supreme Court of Oregon heard the case again and reached the same conclusion.[14]

At the age of 24, E.T. Barnette went to prison. He entered the Oregon Penitentiary on April 21, 1887. It appears that his family back in Ohio petitioned the governor to give him a pardon or commute his sentence. His family was said to have the aid of Governor Foraker of Ohio, whose son had been a boyhood friend of Barnette's.[15] Their efforts were successful, and after Barnette had spent one year, three months, and four days in prison, he walked out a free man. The reasons and conditions stated on the governor's commutation were: "Former good reputation and unimpeachable standing, doubts as to his guilt, uniform good conduct, sentence is commuted on the express condition that he leaves the State and remain away therefrom forever."[16]

At the age of 25 there were worse fates than to be banished forever from the state of Oregon. But Barnette had not yet finished paying for his conviction. The discovery that Captain Barnette had spent time in the Oregon Penitentiary was a shock in Fairbanks. Barnette's enemies made good use of the scandal. The anti-Barnette newspaper, the *Fairbanks Daily Times*, ran a huge, black, one-word headline the day after the captain's confession in Seattle:

EX-CONVICT

Underneath the headline in a black box was the story of the "startling expose" in the Seattle courtroom. "Seattle is all agog over the sensation," the story continued, "and the principal talk where Alaskans hold forth is the Barnette trial."[17]

Reaction against the malicious way the *Times* tried to disgrace and expose Captain Barnette was immediate. At Barnette's bank, friends were calling every hour to express their sympathy for "the attacked absent man."[18] There was talk of a libel suit and worse

The NEWSPAPER of Alaska · **Fairbanks Daily Times** · The PAPER THAT STANDS for RIGHT

VOLUME II.   FAIRBANKS, ALASKA, WEDNESDAY, NOVEMBER 22, 1908.   WHOLE NUMBER 190

EX-CONVICT

AS BAD AS THE WHALING MEN

SCHOONER OAKLAND ARRIVES IN SEATTLE WITH AWFUL STORY FROM SIBERIA.

WHISKEY THE SOLE CAUSE

In court in Seattle yesterday, Capt. Barnette at first denied but when the records were produced admitted, that he had served time in the penitentiary at Salem, Oregon, in 1886. He had been sentenced to four years for the larceny by bailee of $2000, but sentence was commuted to eighteen months by the governor.   The plaintiff says he will show that the names used by Barnette in staking by power of attorney or by proxy, were those who signed the petition for pardon.

THREATEN TO KILL TILLMAN

SENATOR RECEIVES LETTERS WARNING HIM NOT TO MAKE ADDRESS.

NEGROES APPEAL TO MAYOR

*Living Witness Comes From
Intended Death to Testify*

The one-word headline informs Fairbanks readers that the founder and mayor of their town has served time in an Oregon penitentiary for larceny. Barnette's past, until then a closely kept secret, confirmed many of the mayor's detractors in their opinion of him.

(University of Alaska Archives)

against Captain L.B. Anderson, owner of the *Times*, and an enemy of Barnette's.

"We appreciate deeply the fact," the *Tanana Miner* said, "that there is no depth in the filthy sewer of life into which the *Times* will not descend in search of slime to hurl at those the *Times* dislikes."[19]

Captain Anderson replied that he was just doing his duty in reporting all the news. As he explained, "While Mr. Barnette's confession confirmed the opinion that many here in the Tanana held of him, personally, there are higher and better considerations involved in the present case than the mere coarse story of a crime."[20]

The *Times'* defense of "higher and better considerations" was too much for the *Tanana Miner*, then partly owned by Captain Barnette:

We will grant to the Times its right to speak in the name of degeneracy, revenge and crime, for as their champion it had no equal in the Fourth Estate. We will grant to the Times the justice of its title to represent all that is leprous and gangrened in character or society. But, we as strenuously oppose the attempt of the Times to filch from the form of pure decency the honorable veil that shrouds it and wrapping that veil about its slime-covered, leprosy-eaten remains, steal the voice and the attitude of pure decency and peddle its polluted breath . . . in the name of the real purity and decency.

The editor of the *Miner* thought of the words which Antony spoke over the slain Caesar, and warned that such would be the fate of the owner of the *Times*: "But yesterday the word of Caesar might have stood against the world; now lies he there, and none so poor to do him reverence."[21]

Though the news of Barnette's previous troubles with the law were proof of his dirty character to his enemies, the EX-CONVICT story was passed off by his friends as something that had happened 20 years earlier when he was just a young man. His friends argued that everyone has done something or other which he would like to keep hidden; that was the way of the frontier. Captain Barnette's past should belong to himself.

Judge Wickersham worried about the effect the scandal would have on his standing as a judge. Wickersham said he was sure that his enemies "will of course try to damn me with my alleged friendship for Barnette." He wrote sadly in his diary, "We all have skeletons in our closet."[22]

Charges of fraud and corruption in Wickersham's district, brought largely by those against whom the judge had ruled, were investigated again and again, with Wickersham cleared of wrongdoing each time. On four occasions he was given recess appointments by President Teddy Roosevelt because the Senate failed to confirm his nomination. But Wickersham's days as a district judge in Alaska were soon to be over. In September of 1907 Wickersham sent in his letter of resignation to President Roosevelt and gave up his disputed judgeship. The judge had given up ever being peacefully reconfirmed by the Senate, and his wife was ill. So he decided to go back into private practice. His retirement did not last long, though. Eight months after he stepped down, Wickersham was elected Alaska's lone Delegate in Congress, a job he held off and on for a dozen years.

Wickersham's last day as judge was December 31, 1907. He had just decided not to take up Barnette's long-standing offer to become the captain's partner, or to work for him. Instead, he would open his own law practice. Looking back at his seven and a half years on the bench, he was pleased with his record but also a little bitter. He wrote in his diary on his last day, "no one has yet accused me of a graver crime in connection with decisions than favoring Barnette!! A silly charge — Easily made, hard to prove and still harder to disprove! so I'll not try it."[23]

On one occasion, however, when Wickersham was still battling to keep his judgeship in the "hardest fight" of his life, E.T. Barnette was one of his closest allies.[24] In January, 1906, Barnette and his top lawyer, John L. McGinn, were in Washington. From the capital they telegraphed Wickersham in Fairbanks, telling him to come at once but giving no explanation. By boat and train the judge raced to the national capital in seven days and checked in at the Raleigh Hotel. In a somber mood on his first night after arriving in Washington, he wrote in his diary about midnight, "I am up against the hardest fight of my life with a packed subcommittee of the Senate Committee on Judiciary — Senator Nelson is making the most bitter and malicious personal fight against me — but thank Clark, Barnette, McGinn, and others, Bailey and a number of the strongest men in the Senate are for me."[25] The political center of Alaska stretched from the White House to Capitol Hill. Since Alaska had no legislature and its governor was appointed by the executive branch, Alaska was controlled from Washington, D.C., through federal appointments such as Wickersham's.

When Judge Wickersham and Captain Barnette walked down Pennsylvania Avenue shortly after the turn of the century talking Alaska politics, Theodore Roosevelt was in the White House, and his vice-president was Charles W. Fairbanks, the former senator from Indiana.[26]

Though Vice-President Fairbanks eventually went into the historical oblivion of most vice-presidents, Fairbanks did exert considerable influence in his post, and he was attentive to the needs of his friends who had named the largest city in Alaska after him. Had he been President or perhaps a leader in the House or the Senate, Fairbanks might have been too busy to pay much attention to Fairbanks, Alaska. But as vice-president, he had a less rigorous schedule. Besides sending regular holiday greetings to the people in Fairbanks, the vice-president had many powerful friends in the Senate, and a direct line to the President, which he could use to push through appointments or Alaska legislation.

President Theodore Roosevelt sits with his vice-president, Charles W. Fairbanks, who proved a valuable friend to the Alaska town named in his honor. (Library of Congress)

While Wickersham was fighting to be confirmed by the Senate in 1906, Captain and Mrs. Barnette and Judge Wickersham were invited to a private dinner at the home of Vice-President Fairbanks. Wickersham was especially thrilled at the invitation. He was only sorry that he did not have a dress suit with him and would have to wear his Prince Albert coat. He described the affair as "the most elegant dinner I ever attended." Ten people were there, including Vice-President and Mrs. Fairbanks, who sat at either end of the table, as well as Captain and Mrs. Barnette, Former Speaker of the House J.W. Keifer, the judge, and a few others. When dinner was over, the men retired to the library to smoke their cigars, while the ladies went into the parlor.

Former Speaker Keifer had been a general with the U.S. Army in Cuba during the Spanish American War, and he told Wickersham stories about the war and the ravages of yellow fever.

Barnette talked with the vice-president about Alaska. Wickersham, listening on the side, was pleased to hear that the captain was explaining the judge's problems with the Senate. The two gentlemen from Alaska were no doubt equally impressive with their stories of the Far North, especially Captain Barnette's explanation of how he had come to establish the city of Fairbanks.

After finishing their cigars, the men rejoined the ladies in the parlor, and later the group looked at pictures of Alaska and Fairbanks, which Barnette had brought along. The Barnettes presented the vice-president with a large $130 gold nugget, which had been found on Cleary Creek. Wickersham said it was an evening he would never forget.[27]

After Judge Wickersham and the rest of Fairbanks learned that their town father was an ex-convict, things were never the same. And in Washington there were no more after-dinner cigars for Wickersham and Barnette in the vice-president's library. Even before the EX-CONVICT scandal broke in November, there were

E.T. Barnette on his horse, with a gold train in front of his Fairbanks Banking Company. (Courtesy of Thomas McGinn Smith)

at least two people who knew well about Barnette's record years earlier in Oregon. One of them was John L. McGinn, Barnette's lawyer and brother of Henry McGinn, the Portland attorney who had prosecuted the case against Barnette. The other man who had known Barnette in Oregon was now a United States senator. Twenty years earlier Senator John M. Gearin from Oregon had been E.T. Barnette's defense attorney in the case.

The Causten suit against Barnette was going to cause him far more trouble than merely exposing his past. The suit was one reason Barnette's bank was forced to close its doors for a short time in 1907 and almost went out of business. Barnette and Causten were playing an intricate chess game in the courts, with a large part of Barnette's fortune as the stakes. When Causten heard a rumor that Barnette was preparing to sell his Alaska property for 10 cents on the dollar and invest all his money in Mexico, where the suit could not touch it, Causten secured an order from the Superior Court judge in Seattle restraining Barnette from disposing of any of his property. Barnette had reportedly advertised to sell a group of claims on Vault Creek worth about $5 million for $500,000, and the judge's order restrained him from selling these or any of the rest of his holdings.[28] There were other rumors that the only reason Barnette was investing in Mexico at all was to evade Causten's suit. But Barnette scoffed at them and said he was sure he was going to win the case.

Captain Barnette, however, did not win the case. The court ruled that Barnette and Causten had made a verbal agreement in 1902 to "continue their partnership pending accounting of the business" by Barnette to Causten.[29] The court ordered Barnette to give a full accounting, and he was required by the judge to produce the journals and ledgers of the Fairbanks Banking Company and personal records of his own property, his wife's property, and that of his bank partners as well. The court had ruled that Causten and Barnette were partners, but the real question that would not be settled for more than another year was how much money Barnette had to pay Causten.

Causten's attorneys learned of a $200,000 shipment of gold bullion from the Fairbanks Banking Company, which one of Barnette's partners, R.C. Wood, took to Seattle in early December, 1907. The $200,000 in gold was to be deposited with the Scandinavian American Bank in Seattle, partly in repayment of an $80,000 loan. The security Barnette had given for the loan was 96 shares of stock of the Gold Bar Lumber Company, valued at $200,000. Causten's attorneys wanted to make sure that the bank could not release the Gold Bar Lumber Company stock, and they had the judge issue a restraining order freezing the gold shipment so that it could not be accepted in exchange for the stock.[30]

When the news of the freeze on the gold shipment was learned in Fairbanks, depositors in Barnette's bank were frightened that the bank would go under. The scare started a run on the bank. One of those who took his money out of Barnette's bank, when he first heard that the bank was in trouble, was Judge Wickersham. The judge withdrew $5,304.50, his entire account, from the Fairbanks Banking Company on the morning of December 10.[31] Many others pulled out their money as well; and nine days after the announcement of the freeze on the $200,000, the Fairbanks Banking Company closed its doors.

Besides the freeze on the gold shipment, the nationwide panic of 1907 also contributed heavily to the suspension of Barnette's bank. Several large banks and trust companies in New York had failed in October, and a wave of bank closures had spread across the country. Too many people wanted to withdraw their money at the same time, and the shortage of currency was felt everywhere. The Causten case and the nationwide uneasiness sparked the run on Barnette's bank. After nine days it simply had no more cash on hand to give to those who wished to withdraw their money. On December 17 the bank doors were locked with a notice saying that the bank had "temporarily suspended."[32]

Captain Barnette gave a long statement published in both daily newspapers explaining the history of the bank and claiming that the suspension was due to the financial panic in the rest of the country and the "false" reports about the Causten suit published in the *Fairbanks Daily Times*. Barnette promised that everything would be all right, and he added, "I pledge to each depositor my private property to meet the payment of each and all of them in full." The captain did not add that since his bank was a partnership and not a corporation, he and his two partners were responsible (by law) for all the money the bank owed its depositors — almost half-a-million dollars.[33]

Barnette's Fairbanks Banking Company was unincorporated and unregulated. In those times a man with some capital could open a private bank as easily as a saloon or a restaurant, and his business transactions were confidential.

Reasons for the closing of the bank were hotly debated by desperate people who were furious at Barnette. The *Fairbanks*

Daily Times answered Barnette's "false and malicious statement" and gave what it claimed were the real reasons for the failure of the bank. The *Times* believed the main cause of the bank's troubles was Barnette's devious practice of spending the money of his depositors as if it were his own, with no concern for those who had trusted him with their life savings. In three years of operation, the *Times* estimated, Barnette's bank must have made a profit of nearly $400,000. The newspaper asked, "Where has the money gone?" Where did Barnette get the money for his stock farm in Kentucky, his land in Mexico, his big cars Outside, and expensive way of life? How could he afford the huge legal fees that went with spending much of his life in a courtroom, continually involved in one legal dispute or another? Where did the money come from to keep his newspaper, the *Fairbanks News*, publishing when it was common knowledge that the paper was losing more than $50,000 a year?

Answering its own questions, the *Times* said, "All these sums of money came from the Fairbanks Banking Company."[34] In the opinion of the newspaper, Barnette had stolen hundreds of thousands of dollars from the despositors of the Fairbanks Banking Company, and all the land, horses, cars, and the rest of Barnette's so-called "personal fortune" belonged to the depositors of the bank. No one knew exactly how he had done it, but somehow the captain had milked the bank dry.

The Fairbanks Banking Company was closed only for about a week before it reopened its doors, giving out scrip instead of cash. A month later it became an entirely new bank, called the Fairbanks Banking Company, incorporated under the laws of Nevada. Though the bank had the same name, the reorganization made it a corporation instead of a partnership, with Barnette and his partners no longer personally responsible for its debts. Several of the biggest depositors became members of the board of directors of the new corporation, and their names were put up in lettering on the bank's windows. It was as if the Fairbanks Banking Company had been reborn and was starting over again.

Faith in Barnette's bank was buoyed by the reorganization and the appointment of a board of directors, all of whom were leading citizens in the community and had been heavy depositors in the old Fairbanks Banking Company. The fact that the other two banks in town, the First National and the Washington-Alaska Bank, had both gone on a scrip basis because of the shortage of cash convinced many depositors that the temporary closing of

Barnette's bank was due to the nationwide panic and not to mismanagement. Many others would later say that the reorganization of the bank and the new board of directors were only decorations in the window and that from this time forward Barnette's bank was never again solvent.

Not only was Barnette having trouble with the bank and with the Causten suit, but he was also involved in a two-year fight over mining ground near Fairbanks that ended in the attempted murder of one of his partners and had the captain fearing for his own life.

The Dome Creek Mining case was the longest and most complicated legal battle ever fought in the early days of Fairbanks, and Captain Barnette was right in the center. The litigation concerned eight mining claims on Dome Creek which had been staked in 1905 by Henry Cook and Jack Ridenour as an association claim of 160 acres. In the association with Cook and Ridenour were six absent locaters whose names were supplied by Captain Barnette. One unusual aspect of the dispute was that people accused Barnette of giving Ridenour and Cook six made-up names to secure the property for himself. But the six names turned out to be those of Barnette's relatives in Ohio, who had given him their power of attorney. In return for staking claims in the names of his relatives, Barnette received a half-interest in everything he staked. He was actually the largest single claim owner, with half the 120 acres he had staked for his relatives, though his name did not appear as one of the locaters on Dome Creek. Since the maximum area one person could have in an association claim was 20 acres, Barnette had made out pretty well by getting 60. A higher court later ruled that this was fraud on the part of the captain.[35]

A long-standing debate over what constituted a discovery of gold was the basis of the dispute. Before Barnette and company had staked their association claim, several individual miners had staked the ground included in the Dome-Group 160-acre claim. Working for Barnette, Cook and Ridenour had restaked the creek, claiming that a discovery of gold on bedrock was necessary to locate a valid mining claim. The first miners had made what were called muck discoveries, simply finding gold in the dirt at the surface. They had not sunk shafts to bedrock. Judge Wickersham sided with those like Barnette who believed in bedrock discovery, while others said the entire issue was a smoke screen to rob poor miners of their claims.

Barnette and his associates brought suit in court asking that the earlier muck discovery claims be thrown out, but District Judge

Royal A. Gunnison from Juneau, who came to hear the case, disallowed Barnette's suit and ruled that a muck discovery was indeed valid. The map of the claim ownership of Dome Creek was confusing because the boundary lines of overlapping claims and fractional claims were constantly changing. Since the court could not seem to make a final decision on which type of discovery was necessary, the situation grew ever more complicated.

Because there was no clear picture of who owned what, serious arguments were bound to arise. And since the Dome Creek claims were known to be worth several hundred thousand dollars, the legal dispute in the courts was likely to explode into violence on the claims. Trouble started when in August of 1908, Barnette and Jack Ridenour hired several men to dig in a mining shaft on No. 1 Below Discovery. Twenty feet away from the shaft in which Barnette's men were working, four men, two of whom had rifles, started digging another hole. Jack Ridenour walked over and ordered the men with rifles, led by William "Caribou Bill" Deetering, to get off the premises. Deetering had recently purchased a one-quarter interest in the claim and said he had a right to mine the ground. Ridenour and Deetering had words over who had the right to this claim. Then Deetering stepped aside, still carrying his rifle, while Ridenour took a pick and shovel from two of Deetering's men and started walking away. "Caribou Bill" ordered him to drop the tools and fired a shot in the air. When Ridenour did not stop, Deetering put a shell in his rifle and shot him in the back.[36]

Initially, Ridenour was not expected to live. He did survive but became a cripple for life, while "Caribou Bill" Deetering was brought to trial and acquitted.[37] Miners threatened that Barnette would be the next one to get a bullet. They charged that Barnette was nothing but a claim jumper behind the legal monkey business of the bedrock-discovery issue and was stealing the honestly recorded muck-discovery claims of hard-working, poorer men. Less than a month after the shooting, Barnette and his partners signed a contract agreeing to pay out $115,000 to settle the claims. Wickersham wrote that the shooting of Ridenour had "put fear into Barnette who is a moral and physical coward, though a fine specimen of manhood, and threats that he would be next" brought the captain to terms.[38]

September of 1908 was a terrible month for Captain Barnette. Not only was he forced to pay for a clear title to the Dome Creek claims, but he also, finally, had to pay James H. Causten. In an out-of-court settlement the exact terms of which were not made public, Barnette paid the man who had made possible the trip of the *Lavelle Young* a figure somewhere between $125,000 and $200,000. At the time Captain Barnette would admit only that the settlement was "slightly greater than $40,000."[39] Barnette maintained that he would have won the suit eventually and that he settled only to protect his bank. Causten still had several injunctions against the Fairbanks Banking Company, which were dismissed with the settlement. It is impossible to estimate accurately the huge sums paid in legal fees and settlements which Captain Barnette lost in litigation, but Mrs. Barnette later claimed that the Dome Creek case alone cost them half a million dollars.[40]

Virginia (left) and Phyllis (right), the children of Isabelle and E.T. Barnette.

(Courtesy of Jeanette S. Miles)

The money, however, was not the only loss they suffered in these legal battles. Mrs. Barnette and her little girl Virginia had lunch with Judge and Mrs. Wickersham during the fight over Dome Creek. "She is very bitter against those who are fighting her husband," Wickersham wrote, "but I warned her against the cancer of hatred and revenge, that it does those who harbor it more harm than those against whom it is directed." Yet the judge knew how difficult her position was, and he concluded, "Still advice is cheap and cannot change human nature."[41]

Captain and Mrs. Barnette had yet to face the most bitter fight of all, a fight that would doom E.T. Barnette to be remembered only with hatred by the people of the town he had founded.

9

A
White Horse
and a
Dark Night

After settlement of the Causten suit in the fall of 1908, Captain Barnette decided that he wanted to get out of the banking business in Fairbanks. His stock in the bank amounted to $200,000. On the request of the other bank directors, Barnette agreed to leave his money in the bank for at least one year after the Causten settlement to make sure that the withdrawal would not harm the bank.[1]

Barnette wanted to spend more time developing his Mexican ranch. His partner and manager of the ranch, a man named Ward, was working on producing various crops such as corn, barley, tobacco, sugar cane, and cotton. A consultant's report evaluating the worth of Barnette's Mexican holdings and listing the possibilities for future development looked very promising.[2] The plantation was located near the town of San Blas on the Santiago River, northwest of Guadalajara. Because the land was close to a railway and only four and a half miles from the ocean, Barnette had access to cheap transportation to ship his agricultural products to market. The consultant reported that Barnette's hacienda "is well known throughout Mexico as a great producer of fine tobacco," both low grade tobacco for cigarettes and high quality tobacco for pipes and cigars.[3] Some of Barnette's tobacco had previously been sold in Havana.

The outlook for his banana crop was also good. Los Angeles was then using approximately 500 railroad cars of bananas a year, while the people in the Seattle area consumed another 400 cars per year, most of which were shipped from New Orleans. The captain's plantation was 500 miles closer to the big cities on the Pacific Coast than was New Orleans, and seven days nearer by water. The consultant estimated that by planting 3,000 acres of banana trees, Barnette could supply the entire Pacific Coast with bananas, and if the captain purchased three ocean freighters to haul the fruit, he could cut out the middlemen entirely.

The prospects from growing sugar cane were most promising of all. The report declared that for raising sugar cane "there is no better land in the world" than that found on Barnette's plantation. If he planted 6,000 acres of sugar cane, the minimum yield would be 36,000 tons of sugar a year, and if Barnette built his own refining plant he could take in $1.5 million a year from sugar alone. Added to 3,000 acres of bananas and 3,000 acres of coconuts, which together would gross the same amount, the hacienda could bring in at least $3 million a year. This estimate accounted for only two-thirds of Barnette's 18,000 acres in Mexico, and he would be free to develop the rest of the land any way he chose. Some land could go for roads and homes for the workers and the rest for lower value cash crops.

The consultant's report was as optimistic as Barnette in his most expansive mood. The report concluded that Captain Barnette owned fully half of the good delta crop land north of Panama on the Pacific side, and that Barnette's estate was worth at least $400 an acre, for a total value of about $7.5 million, more than the United States government had paid for all of Alaska in 1867.[4] No doubt $7.5 million was an inflated figure, since Barnette himself claimed that the plantation was worth only about $1 million to $2 million or less.[5]

No matter how many millions of dollars the land was worth, Barnette's hacienda, known locally as Canada del Tabaco, was a magnificent estate. On the Mexican holiday of Cinco de Mayo, Barnette's manager staged a huge party for the 600 workers on the hacienda. One practical reason for the party, according to Barnette's manager, was that the nearest town was some distance away. By having a big party on the hacienda, the workers would need only one day off instead of four.

Barnette's manager wrote the captain in Fairbanks describing the celebration. The festivities started between three and four o'clock in the morning with music and fireworks. All the employees from the neighboring haciendas had been invited, and a large crowd was on hand from the beginning. There was eating, drinking, dancing, a parade at noon, and a horse race in the afternoon. The big event of the day was the bullfight at five o'clock. The audience sat in a large grandstand covered with palm branches and watched the banderilleros fight with three young bulls. The fights went off "perfectly without the killing or maiming of a single animal," but the spectacle was not dull as "there were enough bare escapes on both sides to make the affair thoroughly thrilling."[6] After two hours of bullfighting there was more dancing, followed by a traveling theatre company show which lasted until midnight.

Since he believed the native Mexicans were "natural musicians" and loved to play on any occasion, the captain said that when he returned to Mexico in the fall, he would bring a full set of band instruments with him to replace the battered old ones the workers had used.[7]

Captain Barnette no doubt wished that all his troubles could be solved so easily. The banking situation in Fairbanks was less profitable every year. The gold production of the mining camp had apparently peaked. After years and years of steady increases in the total amount of gold mined in the Tanana, the gold output of the 1909-1910 season plummeted by one-third, dropping from more than $9.5 million worth of gold in 1909 to about $6 million in 1910.[8] Even before the bottom fell out of the gold mining industry in Fairbanks, however, the three banks in town were in a desperate three-cornered fight over gold dust. To cut down the competition, Captain Barnette and the men in charge of the Washington-Alaska Bank agreed to buy out the First National Bank. For $125,000 apiece, the Fairbanks Banking Company and the Washington-Alaska Bank each purchased half of the First National Bank in the spring of 1909. The First National Bank continued to operate as a separate institution, but in reality there were only two banks left in town.

In the late summer of 1909, Captain Barnette approached the owners of the Washington-Alaska Bank again and offered to buy them out as well. Barnette explained that he had a plan to "throw all the banks together and sell them to one big bank outside."[9] If Fairbanks had only one bank, Barnette thought, it would be much easier to sell out to a big outside bank for a good price. He made a firm offer of $250,000 for the Washington-Alaska Bank, and the company accepted. The vice-president of the Washington-Alaska Bank at that time was Falcon Joslin, who was also president of the Tanana Valley Railroad. He and his partner, W.H. Parsons, were only too glad to get out of the bank, for they thought it was a losing proposition. Joslin wrote his wife in Seattle on August 23, 1909, and could hardly contain himself:

> Of course you have got my letters about selling the bank before this. I jump with delight everytime the idea occurs to me. . . . There is a terrible spirit of depression here. It is the sense that the camp is over and will decline fast. I hardly think it will go down so very quickly, but go down it surely will and perhaps just drop all at once. It seems everybody is trying to get away. I dread what will be the result when it is known that Parsons and I have sold out the Bank and are going out of the country.[10]

People later accused Barnette of buying the Washington-Alaska Bank with its own money by "means of exchange and intricate bookkeeping." They claimed that at the time he made the purchase his own bank did not have nearly enough money.[11] Whatever the case may have been, Falcon Joslin and W.H. Parsons were certainly glad to sell out. For a short time E.T. Barnette controlled all three banks in Fairbanks, until his old partner, R.C. Wood, exercised a previous option he had on the First National Bank and left Barnette in charge of the Fairbanks Banking Company and the Washington-Alaska Bank.

Captain Barnette's plan to sell the banks of Fairbanks to an outside bank fell through for some reason or another, and he remained as owner. He operated the Fairbanks Banking Company and the Washington-Alaska Bank separately until October, 1910, when the two banks merged into one. The new institution kept the name of the Washington-Alaska Bank.[12] The 1910 season had not been a profitable one, and Barnette claimed that consolidating the two banks would reduce operating expenses and provide a better profit margin. At the same time that the consolidation took place, Barnette secretly submitted a letter of resignation as president of the bank. The letter was not made public for some time. Mrs. Barnette had been in poor health for the past several years; she had given birth to another baby girl in the summer of 1910. The Barnettes had a home in Los Angeles, and the new mother felt she wanted to stay in the California sunshine. So without fanfare Captain Barnette resigned from the bank and moved to California, permanently.

Like Falcon Joslin, Barnette realized that his best days in Fairbanks were over. The gold camp was declining. No doubt Barnette would return to Fairbanks from time to time, since he still owned a large hydraulic mining operation near Circle City, but he would never again be a permanent resident of Fairbanks. The captain was pulling out of Fairbanks in a big way. Later it was alleged that during the two years before Barnette resigned as president of the bank in October, 1910, he had withdrawn at least $731,000 out of Fairbanks and invested the money in California and Mexico.[13]

The *Seattle Times* recognized the significance of Barnette's decision to leave Fairbanks, even though most of the people in the town he had founded did not realize he had left for good. When Barnette arrived in Seattle in the fall of 1910, he announced publicly for the first time that he had resigned the presidency of the Washington-Alaska Bank. The *Seattle Times* covered the story:

> Closing a chapter of his life that is as much an integral part of the history of making a new empire as it is of the story of his own remarkable career, E.T. Barnette, the Seattle-Alaska millionaire banker and mining operator yesterday, by the relinquishment of all his banking interests in Fairbanks, severed his last active business connection with the North.[14]

The *Times* interviewed Barnette and noted that the captain was "content with the riches he has won, and determined to get with them the enjoyment that will serve as the reward for the long hard years of pioneering. . . ." Barnette, at 47, had no plans to sit in a rocking chair. "Having come by his wealth in the prime of life and still being a man of rugged constitution and with a healthy love of outdoor life, Captain Barnette's will not be the usual rich man's retirement." The interview contained an account of the 1907 Panic in Fairbanks, which pictured Barnette as a Little Dutch Boy, singlehandedly stopping a financial crash that could have brought disaster. "No one save a man of known great financial strength and reputation could save the day. Mr. Barnette threw himself into the gap, and by pledging even the gold then being taken from his Dome creek mines. . . . he saved the day."[15]

Captain Barnette usually received favorable press coverage because his life story made good copy. He had seemingly come out of nowhere to found a camp by accident that became the largest city in the nation's largest territory. Now he was retiring with the honor of a champion. An earlier feature article in a Seattle newspaper said Barnette was as "likely to be found hiking across a Mexican mountain with a mestizo for a guide, or hobnobbing in Turkey with a villain Turk, as he is to be found staking some broken prospector. . . ." The captain was a man who had a "way of doing remarkable things in a remarkable way":

> His orbit is along the greater and not the lesser dimension. When his hand reaches out, it is to grasp a mountain and no mole hill, and he has accumulated some few mountains. His route to what he wants is straight across the tundra, and he travels, no matter what the obstacle, human or inert. And he leaves on the trail behind him an array of enemies as well as friends. . . .
>
> Barnette is possessed of three characteristics which stand out preeminently. His first is a way of making friends; the kind that stay for the big show and are on hand when the last goat is got. His second is the gentle art of making enemies; the kind that talk of their hatred in their sleep and do pistol practice in their back yards. His third is the science of making money — and giving it away.[16]

The article declared that Captain Barnette had both more money and more enemies than any man in Alaska. But he underestimated the hatred of his enemies, until disaster struck Fairbanks on January 4, 1911.

Little more than three months after Barnette resigned as president of the consolidated Fairbanks Banking Company/Washington-Alaska Bank, the institution collapsed — holding about $1 million in deposits from the people of Fairbanks. The failure of the bank was a complete shock to everyone in town, except the bank's officers, one of whom admitted that in his opinion the "Washington-Alaska Bank is down and out for all time."[17] He was correct. The doors of Barnette's Washington-Alaska Bank never opened again.

The people of Fairbanks were unanimous in blaming one man for the bank crash: the town's founder, Captain E.T. Barnette.

The direct cause of the bank failure in January, 1911, was the refusal of a large Seattle bank to cover an overdraft of the Washington-Alaska Bank. Barnette, after he had removed his money from the Washington-Alaska Bank and submitted his resignation as president, had refused to honor the bank's annual overdrafts personally as he had regularly done before. As Barnette explained, "I thought it was only right now that there

A crowd gathers in front of the Washington-Alaska Bank to watch the transfer of a gold shipment. When Barnette's bank failed in 1911, it spelled the end for the captain in Fairbanks.

were some stockholders there that owned nearly as much stock as I did . . . to see . . . if they could not make their own arrangements for an overdraft. . . ."[18]

But the underlying cause of the bank crash stretched back several years earlier. The bank owned several hundred thousand dollars worth of stock in the Gold Bar Lumber Company of Washington, which had been sold to the bank by Barnette. The manager of the Gold Bar Lumber Company was a man named A.T. Armstrong, another of the captain's many brothers-in-law. The accusation against Barnette was that in the earliest days of his Fairbanks Banking Company partnership, he had his bank buy stock in his own lumber company at an inflated price, though the lumber company was not a profitable investment for the bank. When the bank was reorganized in 1908, the Gold Bar stock was claimed to have increased in value by $100,000. It was alleged that Barnette kept inflating the value of the Gold Bar stock so that

125

his bank would stay solvent, and that as soon as he resigned, he withdrew his personal security for the stock because he knew it was worth far less than the money he had received for it.

Barnette's bank had, in fact, paid about a quarter-of-a-million dollars more for the Gold Bar stock than it could be sold for a few years later. In 1914 when the receiver of the bank liquidated the Gold Bar stock, which had cost the bank $341,000, the highest bidder would give only $100,000 for it. As the *Fairbanks Daily News-Miner* sadly commented, "At this time, there can be no doubt but that the Gold Bar stock was intended from the start by Barnette as the vehicle by which the money of the people could be taken away from them."[19]

Many other fraudulent schemes were attributed to Barnette. One accusation was that he paid for the Washington-Alaska Bank with its own money — funds he took from the Washington-Alaska Bank after the purchase. He was also accused of trying to deceive the depositors by changing the name of the bank to the Washington-Alaska Bank. In reality, the bank was still the Fairbanks Banking Company/Washington-Alaska Bank incorporated under the laws of Nevada, a different bank entirely from the original Washington-Alaska Bank incorporated under the laws of Washington. When the bank failed, it did not at first appear to be Barnette's Fairbanks Banking Company that had failed but rather the old, reliable Washington-Alaska Bank. Few people realized immediately that there were two different Washington-Alaska banks. The depositors were confused and Barnette did not hurry to clear up any of the confusion.

Immediately after the closing of the Washington-Alaska Bank, the depositors held large public meetings to decide what to do next and how to get their money back. The depositors and their friends thought that Barnette was the man to blame, and they demanded that he return their money. For more than a week after the collapse of the bank, not a word was heard from the captain, who was in Los Angeles. His silence was taken as proof of his guilt.

An editorial in the *Fairbanks Daily News-Miner* spelled out the truth as far as the people of Fairbanks were concerned: "Practically, the failure of the bank can be traced to Captain Barnette personally."[20] The editor of the *News-Miner*, W.F. Thompson, had once been Barnette's partner when the captain was in the newspaper business. But the two were friends no longer. Thompson wrote:

Evidently, from start to finish, the Fairbanks Banking Company was the financial agent whose whole duty it was to advance the private interests and private profits of Captain Barnette. If anyone else profited from their investments in that bank, the fact is not known, while it is known that Captain Barnette grew rich through the manipulation of the bank's affairs. He came here a poor man. By the labor of his brains he has juggled finances, imposed and collected usury, bought 'law' and 'justice,' confiscated 'legally' the mines of the camp, until today he is independently rich.[21]

In the eyes of the people of Fairbanks, Barnette had robbed his own bank with his fountain pen.

The first announcement from the former bank president which proved he was even aware of the bank's troubles came through an interview in Los Angeles, published in a Seattle newspaper. The *News-Miner* reprinted the article from the Seattle newspaper under the headline, "CAPT. BARNETTE IS INDIFFERENT ABOUT FAILURE." The story quoted Barnette as saying, "Had the bank been let alone, it would have paid dollar for dollar. It will recover as soon as the season opens. I am not worrying about it."[22] The story did not convince anyone that Barnete was innocent or that he had any plans whatsoever to try to repay the depositors.

In the weeks following the failure, Barnette was the subject of numerous cartoons in the newspapers. The cartoonists made good use of Barnette's words: "I am not worrying about it." Usually he was caricatured wearing a black-and-white-striped convict's suit and smoking a big, black cigar. One cartoon showed the captain dressed in his penitentiary suit, relaxing in a hammock strung between two palm trees. Above the hammock it said "Los Angeles," and at the bottom was the quote, "I'm not worrying."

The most graphic cartoon of all showed an expensive automobile traveling at high speed, driven by a chauffeur wearing racing goggles. In the background are palm trees and a hand pointing towards Mexico. Stretched out and resting comfortably in the back seat of the car is a familiar figure smoking a cigar and wearing a convict's suit. Stored behind him is a bag marked "Wash. Alaska Dough," and the caption at the bottom reads, "No, He isn't worrying."[23]

For many years, people in Fairbanks remembered the founder of their city as having left town as shown in that cartoon, driving off into the sunset towards the Mexican border with half-a-million dollars of stolen money. Captain and Mrs. Barnette, however, did

"I'M NOT WORRYING"

NO, HE ISN'T WORRYING

After the collapse of his bank, Barnette becomes the most hated man in Fairbanks. His enemies claim that the ex-convict is living it up in Los Angeles, or on his way to his Mexican plantation with half a million dollars stolen from the bank. A newspaper report from Los Angeles quoted Barnette as saying that he was "not worried" about the bank failure.

return to Fairbanks after a long delay, and it was a horrifying experience for both of them. Isabelle Barnette had been seriously ill and in the hospital, but she insisted that the captain postpone his trip to Fairbanks until she could go with him. After a two-week delay, Mrs. Barnette was ready to travel. The trip went wrong from the beginning.

The steamer *Victoria* was almost wrecked twice between Seattle and Cordova. On the second grounding, the captain of the vessel came close to giving the order to abandon ship. The officers told the passengers that the ship was not leaking, but one of the crew members privately told Captain Barnette that the water in the hold was four feet deep. The steamer *Bertha* was only three miles away, and after moving to safe water, the *Victoria* transferred its passengers to her. Once on land again the Barnettes had no easier trip. Travel on the overland trail into Fairbanks was slow and difficult: the snow was deep and the horses had to be continually dug out of the drifts.

When Captain and Mrs. Barnette finally reached Fairbanks in the middle of February, a curious crowd gathered at the stage office to meet them. A reporter on the scene thought that judging by her appearance, Mrs. Barnette had "suffered somewhat in health as a result of the hard trip." Captain Barnette said that the trip had been enough to make anyone nervous. Barnette refused to discuss his plans for the bank. He would only say, "I am here to endeavor to straighten out the affairs of the bank. If such had not been my intention, of course, I would never have come back."[24]

Barnette had made it clear before he left Seattle that he did not think he was responsible for the bank closure. He explained to a reporter before he left for Alaska, "My anxiety to see to it that every man gets his money back is not due to a sense of being bound, or any feeling of responsibility, for I am not culpable nor held in any way. I am anxious to rectify matters because I want to protect the depositors, nearly everyone of whom I know personally, and to clear my name of unjust and libelous charges that have been made."[25] Barnette overestimated his ability to take care of the wrecked bank. He was dealing with desperate people who were afraid they had lost their life savings because of him.

The town welcomed the captain's return: everything would be fine if he was going to give the depositors their money back. If wrongdoing was uncovered and the money was not returned, Barnette was going to feel the "lash of public condemnation."[26] In an editorial entitled *Vox Populi*, the "Voice of the People," the

The thermometer reads 58 degrees below zero in Fairbanks, January 24, 1911, the same month that Barnette's Washington-Alaska Bank failed.
(University of Alaska Archives)

Fairbanks Times commented on Barnette's return and warned him that the people wanted action, not double-talk:

> The Captain has said that he desires to get his bearings before announcing his plans, and there appears to be no good reason why the depositors should deny him that privilege. It may not be amiss at this time, however, to tell the Captain just how things stand here. He may have discovered this already, but the residents of the camp desire that there shall be no misunderstanding.
>
> The public believes that Captain Barnette is largely, if not wholly, responsible for the failure of the Washington-Alaska bank. Whether or not they are justified in this belief is not to the point. It is a condition of mind that will greet the Captain on every hand, until the smaller depositors, at least, have been paid in full, or until Captain Barnette has demonstrated beyond any doubt that others than he are to blame for the closing of the bank.[27]

On March 1, 1911, Captain Barnette stated his plan for settlement of the bank's debts. A standing-room-only crowd of about 210 people jammed into the courthouse to hear the captain's proposal. Many depositors came with notebooks filled with questions they wanted to ask the former president of the bank. Finally, they thought, the depositors would get some answers.

Barnette gave a long statement explaining how he would sell the stock of the Gold Bar Lumber Company and sell some of his private holdings to raise the money to pay off the debts of the bank. He wished to take over the bank himself and claimed he needed at least one year to pay off the debts. In the meantime, Barnette said, he would meet with a depositors' committee to explain the details of his plan.

Shortly after Barnette had finished speaking, Leroy Tozier, one of his lawyers, got up and said that Barnette "felt perhaps if he retired the discussion would be a little more free." The captain and his lawyer quickly walked out the door before the audience realized that Barnette was not going to answer any of their questions. An angry man in the crowd shouted after the captain had left that he felt "Barnette had not acted fairly in leaving before he could be questioned." Hearty applause greeted that remark. The next day the *Fairbanks Times* said, "Putting it plainly, the meeting . . . was a failure in every aspect. . . ." The bank had been closed for nearly two months, and the depositors still had not been given a chance to question Captain Barnette. "The people want to believe in him, but thus far they have not been given the opportunity."[28]

Captain Barnette felt he didn't have to answer to a large, boisterous crowd. "I can't deal with a whole mob," he insisted. Instead, he worked with a seven-man depositors' committee.[29] At first it seemed that Barnette and the committee might be successful. They came to a preliminary agreement whereby the depositors would accept as security the deeds for all of Barnette's property, both in the United States and in Mexico, and the deeds for all of Mrs. Barnette's property as well. The committee wanted to have the deeds for the property in Mrs. Barnette's name because the depositors feared that the captain was covering up his true wealth by putting his land in her name.

Suddenly, however, the negotiations fell through, and the committee returned all of Barnette's deeds to him on March 11. After conferring with its lawyers, the committee concluded that the contract was a voidable one and could perhaps hinder them in the long run in their efforts to recover the depositors' money. They felt the major problem was "the honesty of the intentions of Captain Barnette."[30] Because of the possibility that the captain intended to cheat the depositors out of their money, the contract had to be one that he could not break. The committee rejected the securities offered by Barnette largely "because of the committee's suspicion of the man himself."[31]

Barnette had $50,000 in cash on hand, and the committee wanted him to turn that over to the depositors immediately. Fearing that this would be all it could get from Barnette, the committee pressed hard for the $50,000 — not the deeds or Barnette's promises to pay. But Barnette refused to turn over the cash. He claimed he needed the money to operate his plantation and help straighten out the affairs of the bank.

The mood of the city was an ugly one. Mrs. Barnette later claimed that she and her husband had received many anonymous telephone calls threatening that the captain would be assassinated or their children kidnapped if the bank's money were not returned. "Where they had left friends," an observer later said, "they were confronted with enemies."[32]

While Captain Barnette was bargaining with the depositors' committee, a grand jury was investigating the bank failure. When the grand jury finished its work, it concluded there was not enough evidence to bring any indictments under existing statutes. The jury was dismissed. After that, the threats against Barnette and his family no doubt became more regular. The captain had not been indicted, and it appeared he might get off entirely.

On March 27, 1911, several days after the grand jury had finished reviewing the bank failure, Mr. and Mrs. Barnette secretly left Fairbanks. To avoid their persecutors, Mrs. Barnette later said that she was bundled up and hidden in the freight of the sled so that anyone who saw them would not realize they were leaving town. They sneaked out of town at night with a white horse and a double-ender sled. "CAPTAIN BARNETTE SLIPS OUT IN DARK," the newspaper headlined the next day. The story told as much as was known of his secret departure:

> Taking a white horse and a double-ender last evening, after darkness had settled down on the city, Captain and Mrs. E.T. Barnette started out over the trail with the expectation of overtaking at Byler's roadhouse the Orr stage that left town during the afternoon.
> Three friends, only, witnessed the quiet departure, which was made via back streets until the regular trail was reached at the outskirts of the city.[33]

The way the Barnettes left town "created much unfavorable comment." The *Fairbanks Times* was sure that an effort had been made to conceal their departure, since no one would admit having seen the Barnettes leave and it "appeared to be uncertain at the hotel whether or not Captain and Mrs. Barnette had vacated their rooms."[34]

As the founder of Fairbanks rode out of town with his wife hidden in the sled, both of them rode in fear for their lives. And they both knew it was the end of Barnette's career in Fairbanks.

Three days after the Barnettes left town, another depositors' committee charged Barnette with embezzlement and called for a new grand jury to investigate the bank failure. At a large meeting, 225 depositors gathered to hear the charges against Barnette. The police were standing by in case of trouble because the head of the committee, Dr. Aline Bradley, had been threatened by a man who was reportedly being paid by Barnette. Dr. Bradley said the committee would have to hire a new attorney and accountant, but she said she was certain "that the depositors would be willing to spend a little to send Barnette to the penitentiary."[35]

After he fled that night, Captain Barnette returned briefly to Fairbanks on at least two occasions, and he was not received cordially. In the summer of 1911 he came back to Alaska, and on a visit to his property at Circle City, he was pursued by an angry depositor who took matters into his own hands. The depositor decided he would wait no longer for his money. When he caught up with Barnette's party, he presented his bank book to the captain and demanded his money, or else. The captain gave the man his money.[36]

In late November, 1911, E.T. Barnette was arrested in Los Angeles and charged with embezzling $317,000 from the Washington-Alaska Bank. On November 30, 1911, five years and two days after the EX-CONVICT story appeared in the *Fairbanks Times,* the *Los Angeles Times* headlined, "ALASKA BANKER ARRESTED HERE."[37]

"This blow is a blow in the dark," Barnette told a Los Angeles reporter. "I never expected anything like this." Not everyone was as surprised as the captain supposedly was. James Wickersham, who was then serving as Alaska's Delegate in Congress, had had little to do with the captain for some time. Wickersham was serving his second term in Congress, and the most serious charge brought against him in his re-election campaign in 1910 had been his close association with the captain. When Delegate Wickersham learned of Barnette's arrest in Los Angeles, he noted in his diary, "So, Barnette is on the road to the pen again."[38]

Captain Barnette was released on a minimal $3,000 bail. He explained to the *Los Angeles Times* that he just about had the bank's problems solved, as he was then working out a deal with a London syndicate to sell it 12,000 acres on the west coast of Mexico and thought he would have the bank's debts paid off in four months. He added, as he always did, "I am not legally responsible, or morally, either, for the failure of the bank. . . ."[39]

Not only Barnette but most of the other former directors of the Washington-Alaska Bank were also indicted and charged with embezzlement and falsely reporting the condition of the bank. An entire year of legal challenges and maneuvers passed before Barnette and the other bankers were brought to trial in Valdez in December of 1912.

Captain Barnette had a team of high-priced lawyers, including his friend, Leroy Tozier, T.C. West of San Francisco, Albert Fink of Nome, and five attorneys from Valdez. He needed all the defense he could muster because there were 11 indictments against him for crimes such as making false reports, perjury, conversion, and embezzlement.

Some very unusual testimony was heard during the trials. For example, a perjury indictment against Barnette "went to pieces" when a former attorney of Barnette's testified that even though he had notarized a statement signed by Barnette which contained false information, the captain had not committed perjury because the lawyer did not see him sign the statement and had not put him under oath.

In the end, only one charge against Barnette stuck. He was found guilty of one misdemeanor, making a false report of the condition of the bank with intent to deceive and defraud. The report had been made in September, 1910, when he resigned as bank president. All the other indictments were either dismissed by the court on technical grounds and lack of evidence, or else Barnette was judged "not guilty." Barnette maintained to the end that he was not guilty of the one minor crime of which he had been convicted.

At 10 A.M. on December 28, 1912, Judge Thomas A. Lyons announced, "Stand up, Mr. Barnette. What have you to say why the sentence of the court should not now be pronounced against you?"

"If your honor please," the captain answered, "I should like to make a short statement. To start with I would like to say that I was raised and lived on a farm until I was 21 years old, working on the farm in the summer and attending district school in the winter. In that way my education was a little bit neglected."[40]

The captain continued talking for about an hour, giving the history of his banks in Fairbanks and explaining how he, a poor country boy, knew very little about banking and fully trusted the more knowledgeable men who were working with him. "In conclusion, Judge, I wish to say this, everything that I did in that bank, I thought was right, all the time I was there. As regards the statement of 1909 and 1910, if there was one thing wrong with those statements and I knew it, I hope I never will see my wife and babies again — that is all."[41]

After listening to the "poor country banker" give his final statement "as well or better than any counsel could have stated it for him," the district attorney asked that the maximum sentence of one year in prison be given to Barnette. He urged that the captain should be imprisoned because he was so wealthy that a fine would have no effect on him. The judge said that there were serious doubts in his mind as to the extent of Barnette's guilt and that perhaps the captain had had no criminal motives in filing the report. He fined Barnette $1,000 without costs.

The cases against Barnette were over. Later that day he sailed for Seattle. Captain E.T. Barnette never went back to Fairbanks after his trial in Valdez.

The "rottenest judicial farce the North has ever witnessed," was what the *Fairbanks Daily News-Miner* called Barnette's trial. The people of Fairbanks felt that the captain had bought out justice, as he had bought everything else.

Shortly after the trials were over, the depositors of the Washington-Alaska Bank in Fairbanks hanged and burned three effigies in the city. Two of the dummies represented John McGinn and John Clark, two of Barnette's banking attorneys who, the depositors believed, had been paid to lie on the witness stand. The burning figure in the center was simply marked "Justice."[42]

All of the roughly 1,400 depositors of the Washington-Alaska Bank believed that justice had deserted them. In 1911 before the trials, each depositor had received half of his money back. But it was 16 years before the next dividend was declared in 1927. By the time the receivership of the bank was to be closed in 1934, a quarter million dollars of the bank's assets had been spent on fees and litigation.[43] Doubtless few depositors ever got back much more than half of their money.

The people of Fairbanks never forgave E.T. Barnette. Over the years they forgot the fact that he had been brought to trial for wrecking the Washington-Alaska Bank and acquitted of all but one misdemeanor. The legend of Captain Barnette was that he had skipped town one day with half a million dollars to live out his days in ease and comfort on his ranch in Mexico. The truth is that for many years no one really knew what happened to him.

Epilogue

An old joke in Fairbanks is that appropriately enough, the most crooked street in town is Barnette Street. For years after the failure of the Washington-Alaska Bank, the *Fairbanks Daily News-Miner* used the captain's name as a verb, meaning "to rob." Whenever a bank anywhere in the United States failed or a large sum of money was stolen, the headline might read, "Barnetting Going On Still." The hatred of the frontier con man, however, has dimmed with the years. In 1960 the E.T. Barnette Elementary School was dedicated in Fairbanks, as a gesture of appreciation for a colorful pioneer. Though there were many old-timers who were outraged at the naming of the grade school for a convicted swindler, Barnette was, after all, the town founder, and every year there were fewer people alive who had actually lost money in the captain's bank.[1]

The trail left by Captain Barnette is not an easy one to follow. Except for scattered newspaper accounts, even his days in Fairbanks are rather poorly documented. The captain did not, for obvious reasons, talk about his own past. In all the newspaper interviews and feature stories about Barnette, he never discussed anything that had happened before his trip on the *Lavelle Young* in 1901. In a 1909 edition of the *Alaska-Yukon Magazine*, devoted entirely to the Tanana, a long article gave the biographies of the leading residents of Fairbanks, with their photographs. Included were such people as Felix Pedro; Barnette's brother-in-law, James

E.T. Barnette on the extreme right, standing with the other bankers of Fairbanks behind a shipment of gold they are sending to Seattle.

(University of Alaska Archives, Mary Whalen Collection)

Hill; and three of Barnette's lawyers, John L. McGinn, John Clark, and Leroy Tozier. No biography of Barnette — not even a photograph — was included.

Few pictures of the captain were ever published, and today only a few photographs of Barnette are known to exist. Barnette appears in one group photograph with other Fairbanks bankers, but for years several Alaska pioneers were in disagreement over which man in the group was Barnette. The captain is the heavy-set man with a mustache on the far right, wearing a long fur coat and a fur hat. He is neatly dressed, wearing a tie and a three-piece suit, and standing behind more than a dozen boxes of gold and several Winchester rifles.

In the years after the bank failure, Captain Barnette continued to speculate in far-ranging ventures. In the summer of 1915 the captain reportedly traveled to the Kuskokwim to look over the country with a view to establishing a salmon cannery. But apparently nothing came of this scheme. Kenneth MacArthur, a nephew of Barnette's now living in Seattle, remembers that in about 1916 Captain and Mrs. Barnette stayed with them there for a summer. At that time the Mexican Revolution was still going on, and MacArthur said that Barnette had lost a great deal of money because many of his investments had been expropriated by the Mexican government.[2]

Two years later, in 1918, Mrs. Barnette started divorce proceedings against her husband in a San Francisco court. She claimed that he had been unfaithful to her. By going through the captain's business papers "to satisfy her curiosity," she had found two love letters written to Barnette by a Mrs. Dorothy Pullen of New York. On September 25, 1918, a San Francisco paper printed both love letters under the headline, "Woman's Love For Two Men Revealed in Divorce, Wife Finds Letters Among Her Husband's Papers."[3] The two men Mrs. Pullen was said to have loved were Barnette and his old friend and lawyer, Leroy Tozier, a well-known ladies' man.

A final decree of divorce was granted by the court on January 27, 1920, with Mrs. Barnette getting custody of their two girls, 16-year-old Virginia and 10-year-old Phyllis. The court kept jurisdiction over the captain in case it wished to order him "to contribute to his family's support." Captain and Mrs. Barnette had reached a property settlement, however, and Mrs. Barnette was said to be worth $500,000 in her own right. Some 22 years later, in September of 1942, Isabelle Barnette died in a state hospital in Agnew, California.

At the time of the divorce settlement, the captain was thought to be in Mexico, where he had been plagued by bandits raiding his estate.[4] In the 1920s Barnette was reported "to be in the oil game in Montana."[5] But his main interests continued to be in Southern California and Mexico, and he kept a residence in Mexico City. Barnette received little publicity in his later years, and was rumored to have died in the late 1920s.[6]

When he actually passed away, the newspapers took no notice of his death. E.T. Barnette died in Los Angeles on May 22, 1933, from falling down a flight of stairs and fracturing his skull. He was about 70 years old. The autopsy report said his death was accidental.

In life and in death, Barnette was a mystery. The physician in the LA Coroner's Office who performed the autopsy knew almost nothing about the dead man, and he wrote the word "unknown" on a dozen different blanks on Barnette's death certificate.[7] Perhaps that is the way E.T. Barnette would have wanted it. He was a man who could never afford to look back.

Notes

Chapter 1

1. *Seattle Post-Intelligencer*, 17 July 1897.
2. Ernest Ingersoll, *Goldfields of the Klondike and the Wonders of Alaska* (n.p.: Edgewood Publishing Company, 1897), pp. 15-21.
3. *Seattle Post-Intelligencer*, 20 July 1897.
4. Ibid.
5. *Seattle Post-Intelligencer*, 2 August 1897.
6. *The Official Guide to the Klondyke Country and the Goldfields of Alaska* (Chicago: W.B. Conkey Company, 1897), pp. 55-61.
7. *Tanana Weekly Miner*, 8 February 1907.
8. Pierre Berton, *The Klondike Fever* (New York: Alfred A. Knopf, 1974), p. 137, 208; Lulu Fairbanks Collection, Clipping file, Box 2-Folder 13, University of Alaska Archives.
9. *Tanana Weekly Miner*, 8 February 1907.
10. *Seattle Post-Intelligencer*, 6 August 1897.
11. Ibid.
12. Ibid.
13. *Tanana Weekly Miner*, 8 February 1907.
14. Ibid.
15. U.S. Department of Labor, *The Alaskan Gold Fields and the Opportunities They offer for Capital and Labor*, by Samuel C. Dunham, Bulletin No. 16 (Washington, D.C.: Government Printing Office, 1898), p. 405.
16. Ibid., p. 406.
17. Ibid., p. 407.
18. *Tanana Weekly Miner*, 8 February 1907.
19. Ibid.
20. U.S. Department of Labor, *The Alaskan Gold Fields*, p. 408.
21. *Tanana Weekly Miner*, 8 February 1907.
22. U.S. Department of Labor, *The Alaskan Gold Fields*, p. 410.
23. Ibid., p. 412.
24. Ibid.
25. Ibid.
26. *Yukon Press*, March 1898.
27. *Seattle Post-Intelligencer*, 9 February 1901.

Chapter 2

1. There are many conflicting accounts of Pedro's trip in 1898. All contain some useful information. *Fairbanks Daily Times*, 24 July 1910; *Fairbanks Daily News-Miner*, Special Golden Days Edition, 20 July 1967; "Tanana Gold Fields," Special Edition of the *Fairbanks News*, May 1904; Genevieve Alice Parker, "The Evolution of Placer Mining Methods in Alaska" (B.S. Thesis, Alaska Agricultural College and School of Mines, 1929), p. 7; B.B. Metheany, "Men and Endeavor in the Tanana Valley," *Alaska Yukon Magazine*, January 1909, p. 302.

2. *Fairbanks Daily News-Miner*, Special Golden Days Edition, 20 July 1967.

3. Personal Diary of Judge James Wickersham, University of Alaska Archives, 30 September 1904.

4. Cecil F. Robe, "The Penetration of an Alaskan Frontier, The Tanana Valley and Fairbanks" (Ph.D. dissertation, Yale University, 1943), p. 118.

5. Parker, "The Evolution of Placer Mining," p. 13; Statement of A.A. Everman, "From Dawson to Circle in the Spring of 1900," University of Washington Archives.

6. *Fairbanks Miner*, May 1903. Reprinted in James Wickersham, *Old Yukon* (St. Paul: West Publishing Company, 1938), pp. 210-216.

7. *Daily Klondike Nugget*, 11 October 1901.

8. William R. Hunt, *Arctic Passage* (New York: Charles Scribner's Sons, 1975), pp. 211-215.

9. *Daily Klondike Nugget*, 11 October 1901.

10. Ibid.

11. *Tanana Weekly Miner*, 26 April 1907.

12. *Daily Klondike Nugget*, 11 October 1901.

13. C.W. Adams, "I Hauled 'Fairbanks' on a Sternwheeler," *Alaska Sportsman*, September 1961, p. 14; *Fairbanks Daily News-Miner*, Special Golden Days Edition, 22 July 1952.

14. *Daily Klondike Nugget*, 11 October 1901.

15. Ibid.

16. Adams, "I Hauled Fairbanks," p. 14.

17. *Fairbanks Daily News-Miner*, Special Golden Days Edition, 22 July 1952.

18. *Tanana Weekly Miner*, 26 April 1907.

19. Adams, "I Hauled Fairbanks," p. 14.

20. *Daily Klondike Nugget*, 11 October 1901.

21. N.V. Hendricks, "Synopsis of Princess of the Great Light," Box 1-Folder 4, University of Alaska Archives; *Farthest North Collegian*, 1 October 1935.

22. *Fairbanks Daily News-Miner*, Special Golden Days Edition, 22 July 1952.

23. Adams, "I Hauled Fairbanks," p. 15.

24. *Fairbanks Daily News-Miner*, Special Golden Days Edition, 22 July 1952.

25. Wickersham, *Old Yukon*, p. 182.

26. Adams, "I Hauled Fairbanks," p. 15.

27. Ibid.

28. *Fairbanks Daily News-Miner*, Special Golden Days Edition, 22 July 1952. Some sources indicate that Frank Costa might have been the man with Pedro when he met Barnette. See *Tanana Gold Fields*; C.W. Adams, "I Hauled 'Fairbanks,' " p. 15. The *Fairbanks Miner*'s account of Pedro's meeting with Barnette, however, written in 1903, stated that Gilmore was the man with Pedro.

Chapter 3

1. *All Alaska Weekly*, 16 July 1976.

2. *Daily Klondike Nugget*, 11 October 1901.

3. Ibid.

4. *Daily Klondike Nugget*, 6 April 1903; *Fairbanks Miner*, May 1903.

5. *Fairbanks Miner*, May 1903.

6. *Fairbanks Daily News-Miner*, Special Golden Days Edition, 22 July 1952; David Wharton, *The Alaska Gold Rush* (Bloomington: Indiana University Press, 1972), p. 292.

7. *Fairbanks Daily Times*, 23 February 1907; *Northern Light*, 23 February 1907.

8. *Fairbanks Miner*, May 1903.

9. *Alaska Forum*, 28 December 1901.

10. James Huntington, *On the Edge of Nowhere* (New York: Crown Publishers, 1966), p. 28.

11. *Alaska Forum*, 28 December 1901.

12. *Alaska Forum*, 11 January 1902.

13. *Fairbanks Miner*, May 1903.

14. *Weekly Alaska Prospector*, 10 April 1902.

15.Ibid.

16. *Weekly Alaska Prospector*, 17 April 1902.

17. *Tanana Weekly Miner*, 26 April 1907.

18. Wickersham, *Old Yukon*, p. 38.

19. *Dawson Daily News*, 18 April 1903.

20. Wickersham, *Old Yukon*, p. 141.

21. Ibid., pp. 2-3.

22. Robe, "The Penetration of an Alaskan Frontier," p. 123.

23. Wickersham's Diary, 19 July 1902.

24. *Seattle Post-Intelligencer*, 21 April 1903.

25. *Fairbanks Daily Times*, 15 July 1913.

Chapter 4

1. *Fairbanks Miner*, May 1903.

2. Ibid.

3. *Fairbanks Daily Times*, 28 November 1906.

4. *Fairbanks Miner*, May 1903.

5. Ibid.

6. Wickersham, *Old Yukon*, p. 181.

7. Fairbanks District Records Office, Mining Location Notices.

8. Ibid.

9. R.N. DeArmond, comp., *Stroller White: Tales of a Klondike Newsman* (Vancouver: Mitchell Press Limited, 1969), p. 119.

10. *Seattle Post-Intelligencer*, 13 February 1903.

11. Ibid.

12. Ibid.

13. L.M. Prindle, "Gold Placers of the Fairbanks District," *Contributions to Economic Geology, 1903*, U.S.G.S. Bulletin No. 225 (Washington: Government Printing Office, 1904), p. 69.

14. Parker, "The Evolution of Placer Mining," pp. 20-25.

15. Ibid., p. 25.

16. Robe, "The Penetration of an Alaskan Frontier," pp. 145-146.

17. *Tanana Weekly Miner*, 11 January 1907.

18. De Armond, *Stroller White*, pp. 96-97; *Jessens Weekly*, 21 August 1952.

19. *Yukon Sun*, 17 January 1903.

20. Ibid.

21. Ibid.

22. Ibid.

23. *Daily Klondike Nugget*, 21 January 1903, 26 January 1903.

24. *Daily Klondike Nugget*, 19 January 1903.

25. *Daily Klondike Nugget*, 17 January 1903.

Chapter 5

1. *Daily Klondike Nugget*, 7 March 1903.

2. "History of W.A.M.C.A.T.," *The Pathfinder of Alaska*, (3 parts), March 1925, pp. 5-18, April 1925, pp. 3-21, May 1925, pp. 5-17.

3. William Mitchell, "The Opening of Alaska," p. 158, William Mitchell Collection, University of Alaska Archives.

4. Ibid., p. 158.

5. *Daily Klondike Nugget*, 16 February 1903.

6. *Daily Klondike Nugget*, 24 February 1903.

7. *Daily Klondike Nugget*, 21 February 1903; 23 February 1903; 24 February 1903; 25 February 1903; 16 March 1903; 17 March 1903; *Yukon Sun*, 28 May 1903; *Dawson Daily News*, 7 April 1903.

8. Robe, "The Penetration of an Alaskan Frontier," pp. 145-146.

9. William B. Ballou Papers, letter from Ballou to "Dear Mother," 8 January 1903, Box 2-Folder 129, University of Alaska Archives.

10. *Valdez News*, 14 December 1901.

11. *Yukon Sun*, 17 February 1903.

12. Records of the Bureau of Land Management, Fairbanks District Office, Chena Townsite File TS2-135.

13. *Daily Klondike Nugget*, 6 April 1903.

14. Robe, "The Penetration of an Alaskan Frontier," pp. 148-149.

15. *Yukon Sun*, 21 November 1903.

16. *Dawson Daily News*, 7 April 1903; *Seattle Post-Intelligencer*, 29 March 1903; Abe Spring, "Early History of Tanana Valley," *Alaska Yukon Magazine*, February 1909, p. 261.

17. *Daily Klondike Nugget*, 4 March 1903.

18. *Yukon Sun*, 18 April 1903.

19. *Dawson Daily News*, 11 April 1903.

20. Berton, *Klondike Fever*, p. 319.

21. *Yukon Sun*, 27 February 1903.

22. *Yukon Sun*, 1 March 1903.

23. *Daily Klondike Nugget*, 31 March 1903.

24. Alaska Forum, 28 February 1903.

25. Ibid.

26. *Daily Klondike Nugget*, 18 March 1903.

27. *Dawson Daily News*, 7 April 1903.

28. Robe, "The Penetration of an Alaskan Frontier," p. 168; *Yukon Sun*, 11 April 1903; *Daily Klondike Nugget*, 6 April 1903; T.A. Rickard, *Through the Yukon and Alaska* (San Francisco: Mining and Scientific Press, 1909), p. 266.

29. *Daily Klondike Nugget*, 6 April 1903.

30. *Dawson Daily News*, 30 January 1904; *Daily Klondike Nugget*, 6 April 1903; *Northern Light*, 23 February 1907.

31. *Daily Klondike Nugget*, 6 April 1903.

32. Ibid.

33. Ibid.

34. Ibid.

35. Wickersham's Diary, 16 March 1903-28 March 1903.

36. Wickersham, *Old Yukon*, p. 182.

37. *Fairbanks Daily News-Miner*, 20 July 1955.

38. Wickersham, *Old Yukon*, p. 182.

39. Wickersham's Diary, 10 April 1903.

40. *Fairbanks Record of Deeds*, Vol. 1, p. 168, 187, 284.

41. *Miner's Union Bulletin*, 25 July 1910.

42. *Fairbanks Miner*, 1903.

43. *Daily Klondike Nugget*, 1 July 1903.

44. Ibid.

Chapter 6

1. *Skagway Daily Alaskan,* 9 May 1903.

2. *Seattle Post-Intelligencer,* 9 March 1903.

3. Records of the Post Office Department, RG 28, Box 15, Reports on Site Locations, Alaska Fourth Division.

4. *Yukon Sun,* 27 May 1903.

5. *Yukon Sun,* 28 May 1903.

6. *Northern Light,* 23 February 1907.

7. Robe, "The Penetration of an Alaskan Frontier," pp. 181-182.

8. Harry Badger, Historical Tape Recording, University of Alaska Archives Tape Collection.

9. Robe, "The Penetration of an Alaskan Frontier," p. 183.

10. U.S. Department of Interior, United States Geological Survey, *A Geologic Reconnaissance of the Fairbanks Quadrangle, Alaska,* by L.M. Prindle, Bulletin No. 525 (Washington: Government Printing Office, 1913), pp. 111-112.

11. U.S. Department of Interior, United States Geological Survey, *The Gold Placers of the Fortymile, Birch Creek, and Fairbanks Regions, Alaska,* by L.M. Prindle, Bulletin No. 251 (Washington: Government Printing Office, 1905), p. 77.

12. *Yukon Sun,* 24 November 1903.

13. Robe, "The Penetration of an Alaskan Frontier," p. 183.

14. U.S. Department of Interior, U.S.G.S., Bulletin No. 525, *A Geologic Reconnaissance of the Fairbanks Quadrangle,* pp. 111-112.

15. U.S. Department of Interior, United States Geological Survey, *Methods and Costs of Gravel and Placer Mining in Alaska,* by C.W. Purington, Bulletin No. 263 (Washington: Government Printing Office, 1905), pp. 41-42; *Tanana Weekly Miner,* 1 March 1907.

16. U.S. Department of Interior, U.S.G.S., Bulletin No. 263, *Methods and Costs of Mining,* pp. 96-98.

17. Rickard, *Through the Yukon and Alaska,* p. 272.

18. Ibid.

19. *Valdez News,* 21 January 1905.

20. *Valdez News,* 5 December 1903.

21. Ibid.

22. *Tanana Gold Fields.*

23. Berton, *Klondike Fever,* p. 178.

24. *Tanana Gold Fields.*

25. *Fairbanks Weekly News,* 19 September 1903.

26. *Tanana Gold Fields.*

27. *Fairbanks Weekly News,* 19 September 1903.

28. Fairbanks District Recorder's Office, "Fairbanks Lot Book No. 1."

29. *Alaska Forum,* 26 December 1903.

30. *Tanana Gold Fields.*

31. Ibid.

32. *Dawson Daily News,* 30 January 1904.

33. U.S. Department of Interior, U.S.G.S., Bulletin No. 251, *Gold Placers of the Fortymile,* p. 68; Spring, "Early History of Tanana Valley," p. 261.

34. *Tanana Gold Fields.*

35. Ibid.

36. *Dawson Daily News,* 24 November 1903.

37. Fairbanks District Recorder's Office, "Fairbanks Lot Book No. 1," minutes of city council, 8 December 1903.

38. Julia Bruce, "Schools of the Tanana Valley," *Alaska-Yukon Magazine,* January 1909, p. 265.

39. Fairbanks District Recorder's Office, "Fairbanks Lot Book No. 1," minutes of city council, 2 February 1904, 23 February 1904, 19 April 1904, 5 May 1904.

40. *Fairbanks Weekly News,* 16 April 1904.

41. Ibid.

Chapter 7

1. U.S. Department of Interior, U.S.G.S., Bulletin No. 525, *A Geologic Reconnaissance of the Fairbanks Quadrangle*, p. 112.

2. See photos of Fairbanks in University of Alaska Archives, Historical Photo Collection, Fairbanks.

3. *Yukon World*, 9 October 1904.

4. *Alaska Forum*, 4 March 1905.

5. Ibid.

6. *Dawson Daily News*, 26 January 1904.

7. U.S. Department of Interior, U.S.G.S., Bulletin No. 263, *Methods and Costs of Mining*, pp. 238-249.

8. *Fairbanks Evening News*, 10 August 1906.

9. *Dawson Daily News*, 11 February 1904, 20 February 1904, 5 September 1904; Martin Harrais Collection, "Gold Lunatics," p. 133, University of Alaska Archives.

10. *Dawson Daily News*, 19 August 1904; Harrais, "Gold Lunatics," p. 133.

11. Margaret Harrais Collection, "Alaska Periscope," p. 112, University of Alaska Archives.

12. Wickersham's Diary, 31 May 1904.

13. *Alaska Forum*, 11 June 1904.

14. *Dawson Daily News*, 21 July 1904.

15. *Yukon World*, 30 August 1904; *Skagway Daily Alaskan*, 19 August 1904.

16. *Dawson Daily News*, 15 September 1904.

17. *Dawson Daily News*, 8 October 1904.

18. Duane Koenig "Ghost Railway in Alaska: The Story of the Tanana Valley Railroad," *Pacific Northwest Quarterly*, January 1954, pp. 8-12.

19. *Fairbanks Daily News-Miner*, 12 September 1916.

20. *Directory of the Tanana Valley* (Fairbanks: Tanana Directory Company, 1907), p. 20.

21. *Fairbanks Weekly Times*, 24 February 1913.

22. *Fairbanks Daily Times*, 13 November 1906.

23. "Discovery Saved Capt. Barnett's (sic) Neck," unidentified clipping in scrapbook of Eva Alvey Richards, 1908-1912, University of Alaska Archives.

24. *Fairbanks Daily Times*, 23 February 1907.

25. "Discovery Saved Capt. Barnett's Neck," Richards' Scrapbook, 1908-1912, University of Alaska Archives.

26. *Yukon Valley News*, 17 September 1904; Robe, "The Penetration of an Alaskan Frontier," p. 199; James Wickersham, *Alaska Reports* (St. Paul: West Publishing Company, 1906), pp. 286-292.

27. Wickersham's Diary, 5 May 1904; Jeannette Paddock Nichols, *Alaska* (Cleveland: Arthur H. Clark Company, 1924).

28. Fairbanks District Recorder's Office, "Misc. Book 3, Mining Leases," pp. 11-12.

29. *Tanana Directory*, p. 20.

30. James Wickersham, "Address: At the Driving of the Golden Spike and the completion of the Tanana Mines railway, at Fairbanks, Alaska, July 17, 1905," Alaska Historical Library, Juneau; *Tanana Directory*, p. 20; *Seattle Post-Intelligencer*, 15 August 1905.

31. Ronald Atkin, *Revolution!* (New York: The John Day Company, 1969), p. 20.

32. *Tanana Weekly Miner*, 12 April 1907.

33. *Fairbanks Daily Times*, 19 June 1910, 21 June 1910, 2 February 1911; *Fairbanks Weekly Times*, 3 March 1911, 23 February 1913.

34. *Fairbanks Daily Times*, 22 February 1911.

35. *Fairbanks Daily News*, 20 June 1908.

36. *Dawson Daily News*, 10 July 1905.

37. Ibid.

38. *Alaska Forum*, 15 July 1905.

39. Herbert Heller, *Sourdough Sagas*, (New York: Ballantine Books, 1967), p. 214; *Tanana Directory*, p. 116; *Fairbanks News*, 23 May 1906; *Fairbanks Times*, 23 May 1906.

40. *Tanana Directory*, p. 116.

Chapter 8

1. *Fairbanks Evening News*, 7 August 1905.

2. James Wickersham, "Address: At the Driving of the Golden Spike of Tanana Mines railway," Alaska Historical Library, Juneau.

3. *Seattle Post-Intelligencer*, 27 August 1905.

4. *Fairbanks Evening News*, 7 August 1905.

5. *Tanana Weekly Miner*, 26 April 1907.

6. Ibid.

7. Ibid.

8. Ibid.

9. *Fairbanks Daily Times*, 28 November 1906.

10. State of Oregon v. E.T. Barnett (sic), Circuit Court of Multnomah County, Summary of the facts of the trial, 1886.

11. *Morning Oregonian*, (Portland), 1 November 1886.

12. *Morning Oregonian*, (Portland), 27 November 1886.

13. *Morning Oregonian*, (Portland), 28 November 1886.

14. State v. Barnett (sic), 14 Pacific Reporter, Supreme Court of Oregon, pp. 737-740.

15. Robe, "The Penetration of an Alaskan Frontier," p. 98.

16. Commutation of E.T. Barnette, Oregon State Archives, Governors Record of Commutations, 1878-1903, Vol. II.

17. *Fairbanks Daily Times*, 28 November 1906.

18. *Tanana Weekly Miner*, 6 December 1906.

19. Ibid.

20. Ibid.

21. Ibid.

22. Wickersham's Diary, 27 November 1906.

23. Ibid., 31 December 1907.

24. Ibid., 26 January 1906.

25. Ibid., 26 January 1906.

26. Allen Johnson and Dumas Malone, eds., *Dictionary of American Biography* (New York: Charles Scribner's Sons, 1931), p. 249.

27. Wickersham's Diary, 11 February 1906.

28. *Fairbanks Daily Times*, 31 January 1907.

29. James H. Causten v. E.T. Barnette, King County Superior Court, Seattle, Washington, King County Case No. 50813, "Findings of Fact," 1906.

30. *Fairbanks Sunday Times*, 8 December 1907.

31. Wickersham's Diary, 10 December 1907.

32. *Fairbanks Daily Times*, 18 December 1907.

33. *Fairbanks Daily Times*, 17 December 1907.

34. *Fairbanks Daily Times*, 13 Decmber 1907.

35. Cook et. al. v. Klonos et. al., 164 Federal Reporter, C.C.A., Ninth Circuit, pp. 529-539, 1908.

36. *Fairbanks Daily Times*, 28 August 1908.

37. *Anchorage Daily Times*, 27 March 1919.

38. Wickersham's Diary, 16 September 1908.

39. *Fairbanks Daily Times*, 22 July 1911; *Alaska Weekly*, 4 July 1930; *Fairbanks Daily News-Miner*, 10 September 1908.

40. *Anchorage Daily Times*, 27 March 1919.

41. Wickersham's Diary, 17 June 1907.

Chapter 9

1. *Fairbanks Daily Times*, 22 February 1911.

2. Ibid.

3. Ibid.

4. Ibid.

5. *Los Angeles Times*, 30 November 1911.

6. *Fairbanks Daily Times*, 21 June 1910.

7. Ibid.

8. U.S. Department of Interior, U.S.G.S., Bulletin No. 525, *A Geologic Reconnaissance of the Fairbanks Quandrangle*, pp. 111-112.

9. Letter of Falcon Joslin to his wife, 6 August 1909, author's personal collection.

10. Letter of Falcon Joslin to his wife, 23 August 1909, author's personal collection.

11. *Fairbanks Weekly Times*, 19 April 1911.

12. *Fairbanks Weekly Times*, 22 February 1911.

13. *Fairbanks Daily Times*, 30 March 1911.

14. *Fairbanks Daily Times*, 5 January 1911.

15. Ibid.

16. "Discovery Saved Capt. Barnett's Neck," Richards' Scrapbook, 1908-1912, University of Alaska Archives.

17. *Fairbanks Daily Times*, 5 January 1911.

18. *Fairbanks Weekly Times*, 24 February 1913.

19. *Fairbanks Daily News-Miner*, 2 February 1914.

20. *Fairbanks Daily News-Miner*, 9 January 1911.

21. *Fairbanks Daily News-Miner*, 12 January 1911.

22. *Fairbanks Daily News-Miner*, 13 January 1911.

23. *Fairbanks Weekly Times*, 18 January 1911; 1 February 1911.

24. *Fairbanks Weekly Times*, 22 February 1911.

25. *Fairbanks Weekly Times*, 8 February 1911.

26. *Fairbanks Weekly Times*, 11 January 1911.

27. *Fairbanks Weekly Times*, 8 March 1911.

28. *Fairbanks Daily Times*, 2 March 1911.

29. *Fairbanks Weekly Times*, 24 February 1913.

30. *Fairbanks Weekly Times*, 15 March 1911.

31. *Fairbanks Weekly Times*, 5 April 1911.

32. *San Francisco Examiner*, n.d.

33. *Fairbanks Daily Times*, 28 March 1911.

34. Ibid.

35. *Fairbanks Weekly Times*, 5 April 1911.

36. *Iditarod Pioneer*, 5 August 1911.

37. *Los Angeles Times*, 30 November 1911.

38. Wickersham's Diary, 1 December 1911.

39. *Los Angeles Times,* 30 November 1911.

40. *Fairbanks Weekly Times,* 24 February 1913.

41. Ibid.

42. *Fairbanks Weekly Times,* 13 January 1913.

43. *Fairbanks Daily News-Miner,* 14 May 1934.

Epilogue

1. William R. Hunt, *North of 53* (New York Macmillan Publishing Co., 1974), p. 175; Wharton, *The Alaska Gold Rush,* pp. 238-239.

2. Telephone Interview with Kenneth MacArthur, 12 October 1978.

3. *San Francisco Examiner,* 25 September 1918.

4. *Los Angeles Times,* 28 January 1920.

5. *Anchorage Weekly Times,* 5 February 1921.

6. *Alaska-Yukon Gold Book* (Seattle: Sourdough Stampede Association, Inc., 1930), p. 134. The Gold Book was compiled by the Alaska-Yukon Pioneers and the Ladies of the Golden North in 1929-1930, for the Sourdough reunion held in Seattle in August, 1929. Included in the roster of pioneers was "A Partial List of Departed Alaska and Yukon Pioneers," and the entry: "Barnett, Capt. E.T."

7. *Fairbanks Daily News-Miner,* 16 July 1983; California State Registrar of Vital Statistics, Standard Certificate of Death 33-031745, for E.T. Barnette. Special thanks to Robert King of Fairbanks for uncovering the death certificate.

Selected Bibliography

Archival Sources

1. University of Alaska Archives, Fairbanks
   Harry Badger Historical Tape Recording
   William B. Ballou Papers
   Margaret Harrais Collection
   Martin Harrais Collection
   Nathan V. Hendricks Collection
   William Mitchell Collection, microfilm.
   Eva Alvey Richards, Scrapbooks.
   James Wickersham's Diaries, microfilm.
2. Oregon State Archives
   Gov's Record of Commutations, 1878-1903, Vol. II.

Newspapers

Alaska Forum (Rampart). 1900-1906.
Alaska Weekly (Seattle). 1923-1933.
Anchorage Daily Times. 1919.
Anchorage Weekly Times. 1921.
Daily Klondike Nugget. (Dawson). 1901-1903.
Dawson Daily News. 1903-1905.
Fairbanks Daily News. (scattered issues).
Fairbanks Daily News-Miner. 1909-1967.
Fairbanks Daily Times. 1906-1916.
Fairbanks Evening News. 1905.
Fairbanks Miner. 1903.
Fairbanks News. (scattered issues).
Fairbanks Sunday Times. 1906-1907.
Fairbanks Weekly Times. 1906-1913.
Iditarod Pioneer. 1910-1912.
Los Angeles Times. 1911.
Miner's Union Bulletin (Fairbanks). 1908-1910.
Morning Oregonian (Portland). 1886.
Northern Light (Fairbanks). 1907.
San Francisco Examiner. 1915-1925.
Seattle Post-Intelligencer. 1897-1905.
Semi-Weekly Klondike Nugget (Dawson). 1900.
Skagway Daily Alaskan. 1903-1905.
Tanana Weekly Miner (various locations). 1906-1907.
Valdez News. 1901-1905.
Weekly Alaska Prospector (Valdez). 1902.
Yukon Press (various locations). 1894-1899.
Yukon Sun (Dawson). 1903-1904.
Yukon Valley News (various locations). 1904.
Yukon World (Dawson). 1904-1905.

Books

Alaska-Yukon Gold Book. Seattle: Sourdough Stampede, 1930.

Berton, Pierre. *Klondike Fever.* New York: Alfred A. Knopf, 1974.

Brooks, Alfred H. *Blazing Alaska's Trails.* College: University of Alaska Press. 1953.

Chicago Record's Book for Gold Seekers. Chicago: Chicago Record, 1897.

De Armond, Robert. *'Stroller' White, Tales of a Klondike Newsman.* Vancouver: Mitchell, 1969.

Directory of the Tanana Valley. Fairbanks: Tanana Directory Company, 1907.

Hamlin, C.S. *Old Times on the Yukon.* Los Angeles: Wetzel, 1928.

Heller, Herbert L. *Sourdough Sagas.* New York: Ballantine Books, 1967.

Hunt, William R. *Arctic Passage.* New York: Charles Scribner's Sons, 1975.

_____. *North of 53.* New York: Macmillan Publishing Co., 1974.

Huntington, James. *On the Edge of Nowhere.* New York: Crown Publishers, 1966.

Ingersoll, Ernest. *Gold Fields of the Klondike and the Wonders of Alaska.* Edgewood Publishing Company, 1897.

Kitchener, L.D. *Flag Over the North; The Story of the Northern Commercial Company.* Seattle: Superior Publishing Company, 1954.

Nichols, Jeannette P. *Alaska.* Cleveland: The Arthur H. Clark Company, 1924.

The Official Guide to the Klondyke Country and the Goldfields of Alaska. Chicago: W.B. Conkey Company, 1897.

Quiett, Glenn Chesney. *Pay Dirt.* New York: D. Appleton — Century Co., 1936.

Rickard, T.A. *Through the Yukon and Alaska.* San Francisco: Mining and Scientific Press, 1909.

Schwatka, Frederick. *Along Alaska's Great River.* New York: Cassell, 1885.

Spurr, J.E. *Through the Yukon Gold Diggings.* Boston: Eastern Publishing Co., 1900.

Wharton, David. *Alaska Gold Rush.* Bloomington: Indiana University Press, 1972.

Wickersham, James. *Alaska Reports.* St. Paul: West Publishing Company, 1906.

_____. *Old Yukon.* St. Paul: West Publishing Company, 1938.

Wold, Jo Anne. *Fairbanks: The $200 Million Gold Rush Town.* Fairbanks: Wold Press, 1971.

_____. *This Old House.* Anchorage: Alaska Northwest Publishing Co., 1976.

Periodical Articles

Adams, C.W. "I Hauled 'Fairbanks' on a Sternwheeler." *Alaska Sportsman* September 1961, pp. 14-15.

Bruce, Julia. "Schools of the Tanana Valley." *Alaska-Yukon Magazine.* January 1909, pp. 263-271.

"History of W.A.M.C.A.T." *The Pathfinder of Alaska,* March 1925, pp. 5-18; April 1925, pp. 3-21; May 1925, pp. 5-17.

Koenig, Duane, "Ghost Railway in Alaska: The Story of the Tanana Valley Railroad." *Pacific Northwest Quarterly,* January 1954, pp. 8-12.

Metheany, B.B. "Men and Endeavor in the Tanana Valley." *Alaska-Yukon Magazine,* January 1909, pp. 289-327.

Paige, Sidney. "A Growing Camp in the Tanana Gold Fields, Alaska." *National Geographic Magazine,* March 1905, pp. 104-111.

Patty, Stanton. "Felix Pedro — A Mystery." *Alaska Journal,* Autumn 1971, pp. 11-15.

Spring, Abe. "Early History of Tanana Valley." *Alaska-Yukon Magazine,* January 1909, pp. 259-262.

Government Documents

Prindle, L.M. "Gold Placers of the Fairbanks District." *Contributions to Economic Geology, 1903,* U.S.G.S. Bulletin No. 225. Washington: Government Printing Office, 1904.

U.S. Department of Interior. United States Geological Survey. *A Geologic Reconnaissance of the Fairbanks Quadrangle, Alaska,* by L.M. Prindle. Bulletin No. 525. Washington: Government Printing Office, 1913.

_____. United States Geological Survey. *The Gold Placers of the Fortymile, Birch Creek, and Fairbanks Regions, Alaska,* by L.M. Prindle. Bulletin No. 251. Washington: Government Printing Office, 1905.

_____. United States Geological Survey. *Methods and Costs of Gravel and Placer Mining in Alaska,* by C.W. Purington. Bulletin No. 263. Washington: Government Printing Office, 1905.

U.S. Department of Labor. *The Alaskan Gold Fields and the Opportunities They Offer for Capital and Labor,* by Samuel C. Dunham. Bulletin No. 16. Washington: Government Printing Office, 1898.

Court Records

Causten, James H. v. Barnette, E.T. King County Superior Court, Seattle, Washington. Case No. 50813. King County Courthouse.

Cook et. al. v. Klonos et. al. 164 Federal Reporter. Circuit Court of Appeals, Ninth Circuit, 1908, pp. 529-539.

State of Oregon, v. E.T. Barnett (sic). Records of Circuit Court Multnomah County, State of Oregon.

State of Oregon v. E.T. Barnett (sic). 14 Pacific Reporter. Supreme Court of Oregon, pp. 737-740.

Theses

Parker, Genevieve Alice. "The Evolution of Placer Mining Methods in Alaska." B.S. Thesis, Alaska Agricultural College and School of Mines, 1929.

Robe, Cecil F. "The Penetration of an Alaskan Frontier, The Tanana Valley and Fairbanks." Ph. D. dissertation, Yale University, 1943.

Other Sources

Fairbanks Record of Deeds. Vol. 1. Fairbanks District Recorder's Office.

"Fairbanks Lot Book, No. 1." Fairbanks District Recorder's Office.

MacArthur, Kenneth. Nephew of E.T. Barnette, Seattle, Washington. Interview, 12 October 1978.

Mining Location Notices. Fairbanks District Recorder's Office.

Records of the Bureau of Land Management. Fairbanks District Office. Chena Townsite File — TS2 — 135.

Index

Terrence Cole is a history professor at the University of Alaska Fairbanks and the former editor of the *Alaska Journal*. He earned a Ph.D. in American history at the University of Washington in 1983. He is the author of numerous works on Alaskan history, including *Nome: City of the Golden Beaches* (Alaska Geographic Society, 1984), and has written for *American Heritage, Alaska Magazine, Pacific Northwest Quarterly, Journal of the West*, and other publications.